GUIDE TO
REMODELING
YOUR HOME

Century 21® Editors
and Dan Ramsey

**Real Estate
Education Company**®
a division of Dearborn Financial Publishing, Inc.

4/97

36024117

This publication is designed to provide accurate and authoritative information in regard to the subject matter covered. It is sold with the understanding that the publisher is not engaged in rendering legal, accounting, or other professional service. If legal advice or other expert assistance is required, the services of a competent professional person should be sought.

Executive Editor: Cynthia A. Zigmund
Managing Editor: Jack Kiburz
Interior Design: Lucy Jenkins
Cover Design: ST & Associates
Typesetting: Elizabeth Pitts

Library of Congress Cataloging-in-Publication Data

Century 21 guide to remodeling your home / Century 21 editors and Dan
  Ramsey.
     p.   cm.
  Includes index.
  ISBN 0-7931-2398-4 (pbk.)
  1. Dwellings—Remodeling.   I. Ramsey, Dan, 1945–   . II. Century
21 (Firm)
TH4816.C39   1997
643′.7—dc21   96-52091
                                                                      CIP

Find This Book Useful for Your Real Estate Needs?

Discover all the bestselling CENTURY 21® Guides:

CENTURY 21® Guide to Buying Your Home

CENTURY 21® Guide to Choosing Your Mortgage

CENTURY 21® Guide to Inspecting Your Home

CENTURY 21® Guide to Selling Your Home

CENTURY 21® Guide to Buying Your First Home

CENTURY 21® Guide to a Stress-Free Move

CONTENTS

PREFACE

The only constant thing in this world is change. Jobs change. Families change. Neighborhoods change. People's needs and tastes change.

So it makes sense that homes—the structures that people live in—also must change.

But most folks don't like change. It's difficult, it's costly, and it's uncomfortable. That may seem especially true of changing your home—remodeling.

Actually, change can be fun. It can offer opportunities for growth. It can make life more enjoyable. It can even be profitable. This, too, is true of remodeling.

What can turn remodeling from a worry to a wonderment?

Knowledge!

This book won't show you *exactly* how to rewire a home, but it will show you how to decide what needs to be done—and how to get it done efficiently. In this book, you'll learn all about how to remodel your home. Whether you're thinking of modernizing the kitchen or adding a new bedroom and bath, you'll find lots of knowledge here from those who have successfully remodeled—and lived to tell about it!

First, you'll take a closer look at home remodeling, what it is and what it isn't. You'll see how the remodeling process is supposed to go and what to do when it doesn't. You'll learn new terms as you come to terms with remodeling.

Chapter 2 is about the practical side of remodeling: money. You'll learn how other homeowners have accurately estimated remodeling costs and benefits. You'll also see how they saved money.

Then you'll learn where to get money for your remodeling. Chapter 3 offers proven ideas for financing your remodeling, including tips for getting a loan at the lowest cost. Credit problems? This chapter will show you how to remodel your credit, too.

Are you going to do the remodeling yourself or hire others to do it? Before you decide, read Chapters 4 and 5 of this book. Chapter 4 helps you look at your own skills and decide if the do-it-yourself route is best for you. Chapter 5 offers ideas on how and why to select a remodeling contractor.

It's time to get more specific with your remodeling. The next few chapters will guide you in remodeling your kitchen, your bathrooms, and even changing the size and structure of your home. You'll learn how to remodel existing rooms and add new ones.

You can take your remodeling ideas outdoors. Chapter 10 includes dozens of ideas on how to remodel your yard with fences, decks, landscaping, and other elements.

Are you wired for the Internet? If not, Chapter 11 may entice you to "surf" the Net or otherwise use a computer to help with your remodeling projects. You'll learn how to get online, where to look for information, and what to do with it. Even if you're not ready to go online, this chapter will give you some fascinating information on how it is done.

Finally, a helpful Appendix and a comprehensive Glossary of remodeling words finish out this book. Refer to these sections any time you need clarification on a specific term or resource group.

Along the way, you'll find Money-$aving Tips to help you keep remodeling costs down and get more for your buck. In addition, at the end of each chapter, you'll learn how remodelers can help—even if you're going to do it yourself. And each chapter ends with answers to some commonly asked questions about home remodeling.

Change is good!

All of us in the CENTURY 21® System—*the* source for homeowner information and services—wish you the best in turning your house into your dream home or a special home for its next owners.

CHAPTER 1

Understanding Home Remodeling

Changing lifestyle trends in America today are driving the remodeling boom. As our population ages, elderly parents are moving in with their adult children. This creates the need for more usable living space as three generations often now live together in the same house.

Changes in the way corporate America does business are another factor many people consider when deciding whether or not to remodel. Companies no longer move executives from city to city with each promotion. The home purchased 10 or 15 years ago may no longer suit today's lifestyle, but there's no desire to leave a good neighborhood and location.

Companies are also downsizing and outsourcing, creating a growing need for home office space. Millions of today's homes are also home to a business.

Whatever the reason, you can increase the value of your home and recoup a significant part of the investment if the project is well designed.

What kind of remodeling is typical or worthwhile?

A recent industry survey says that 21 percent of people considering remodeling are planning a kitchen remodeling project. Another 18 percent of remodeling jobs are to add living space to the home. Third on the list, at 11 percent, is bathroom renovations.

Is remodeling profitable?

Depending on the type of project, where the home is located, and the timing of the project in relation to the sale of the home, homeowners may turn a profit from their remodeling job. The national averages for cost recouped within one year of completion are 104 percent for minor kitchen remodeling and 98 percent for a bathroom addition. Add to these the nonmonetary profits of remodeling, and, yes, remodeling can be very profitable.

This first chapter will get your remodeling off on the best start with good planning. It will cover the basics of home construction and remodeling, with emphasis on simple remodeling tasks that offer the greatest financial and aesthetic return on investment.

In the coming pages, we'll look at how homes are built, types of remodeling, and reasons to remodel. We'll also consider popular remodeling projects. Along the way, you'll learn some Money-$aving Tips and suggestions on how your remodeler can help you make good decisions. Finally, we'll answer some commonly asked questions about remodeling.

Understanding Home Construction

Before you start tearing out walls and moving fixtures, you'd better know some more about home construction!

Actually, homes are constructed with a balance of logic and efficiency. They are designed and built to keep cold and critters out while they let sunlight and friends in. There's a logic to home construction that can be easily understood.

How Homes Are Built Today

Today's homes are typically built in systems, each with its own function. For example, a foundation system keeps the house from sinking into the ground under its own weight. The plumbing system distributes water and collects and removes waste. The heating system produces and distributes heat. The framing system holds the house together (see Figure 1.1).

Though the systems in modern homes are similar to those in homes of a century ago, they are not the same. A turn-of-the-century home probably didn't have electrical wiring and may not have had indoor plumbing. A modern home may be prewired for cable TV or even computer networks—systems unheard of just a couple of decades ago.

Wood Frame Homes

Today's homes are usually constructed of wood, and most of what is called dimensional lumber. Some homes are built of logs or timbers utilizing larger wood components, but the vast majority of modern homes are built of 2 × 4s and 2 × 6s. Why?

Efficiency and economy. Large pieces of good wood are harder to find and are thus more expensive than smaller pieces. In addition, smaller pieces are easier to transport, store and install. Modern home construction techniques can be used to build a house faster and more efficiently of dimensional lumber than from logs or timbers. It's also easier to install other systems—heating, electricity, plumbing—in hollow walls of dimensional lumber than in solid wood walls.

Some modern homes have exteriors of vinyl, brick, masonry, or other materials, but, in most cases, the home's frame is of dimensional lumber.

FIGURE 1.1 Components of a Modern House

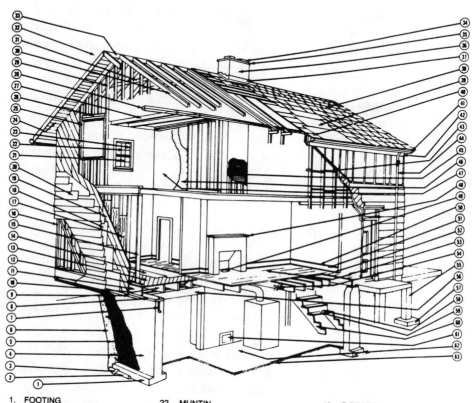

1. FOOTING	22. MUNTIN	43. FIRESTOP
2. FOUNDATION DRAIN TILE	23. WINDOW SASH	44. DOWNSPOUT
3. FELT JOINT COVER	24. EAVE (ROOF PROJECTION)	45. LATHS
4. FOUNDATION WALL	25. WINDOW JAMB TRIM	46. PLASTERBOARD
5. DAMPPROOFING OR WEATHERPROOFING	26. DOUBLE WINDOW HEADER	47. PLASTER FINISH
6. BACKFILL	27. CEILING JOIST	48. MANTEL
7. ANCHOR BOLT	28. DOUBLE PLATE	49. ASH DUMP
8. SILL	29. STUD	50. BASE TOP MOLDING
9. TERMITE SHIELD	30. RAFTERS	51. BASEBOARD
10. FLOOR JOIST	31. COLLAR BEAM	52. SHOE MOLDING
11. BAND OR BOX SILL	32. GABLE END OF ROOF	53. FINISH MOLDING
12. PLATE	33. RIDGE BOARD	54. BRIDGING
13. SUBFLOORING	34. CHIMNEY POTS	55. PIER
14. BUILDING PAPER	35. CHIMNEY CAP	56. GIRDER
15. WALL STUD	36. CHIMNEY	57. FOOTING
16. DOUBLE CORNER STUD	37. CHIMNEY FLASHING	58. RISER
17. INSULATION	38. ROOFING SHINGLES	59. TREAD
18. BUILDING PAPER	39. ROOFING FELTS	60. STRINGER
19. WALL SHEATHING	40. ROOF SHEATHING	61. CLEANOUT DOOR
20. SIDING	41. EAVE TROUGH OR GUTTER	62. CONCRETE BASEMENT FLOOR
21. MULLION	42. FRIEZE BOARD	63. CINDER FILL

As you remodel your home, you may need to change or add to its framing. Later chapters of this book will guide you in making these changes.

Modern Electrical Systems

Few people living today remember homes without electricity. Fewer still would live in a home without this modern necessity. Electricity powers the conveniences that make life easier and more enjoyable.

Because our dependency on electricity has increased over the past century, electrical systems in newer homes are larger and more complex. Older homes may have just one outlet per room. Today's homes usually have at least one electrical outlet per wall. Air conditioners, especially, require more electricity than older cooling systems. In fact, yesterday's homes typically had 100 amps (amperes) of electrical service, while today's homes require 200 amps or more.

Electrical service comes from the power company through wires down your street. Older neighborhoods have above-ground electrical service, usually strung between poles, while newer areas have underground electrical wiring. The 220-volt electrical service enters through a service head and then into the home through a service box. It is then distributed through house wiring throughout the house. Electrical stoves, heaters, and clothes dryers get 220-volt electrical service, while everything else gets 110-volt service. Most 110-volt electrical service is run through walls and floors using three wires wrapped together in plastic.

So what?

As you plan your remodeling jobs, you must consider changes to electrical service. Adding a room means adding electrical service and wiring to that room. We'll cover what and how in Chapter 9.

Modern Plumbing Systems

We have come to rely on good indoor plumbing systems in our homes and cannot imagine living otherwise. Many remodeling jobs require adding or upgrading the home's plumbing system. So it is important to know how it works.

Residential plumbing systems are actually two systems: water and waste. The water system distributes water from a municipal system or a well to the plumbing fixtures within the home: sinks, toilets, tubs, showers, hot water heater, etc. Water pressure from the source pushes the water through your home's water distribution system.

The waste system collects used water and sends it off to a municipal sewage treatment plant or to your home's septic system.

As you can imagine, the two plumbing systems must be completely separate from one another. Waste cannot be allowed to contaminate the fresh water system.

☞ **Money-$aving Tip #1** *Modern plumbing systems rely on plastic or PVC pipes to distribute water and to collect waste. Plastic pipes are not only less expensive than metal pipes, they are also easier to install and so are used in most modern homes. Even if your home now has copper or other metal pipes, you can use plastic pipes for most remodeling jobs.*

Modern Heating and Air-Conditioning Systems

Most modern homes require either heating or cooling or both. In the northern states, heating is vital during winter months, just as cooling is needed in most southern states during the summer. Depending on your home's heating and cooling needs, the systems can be combined into one year-round system called a comfort control system.

Heating and cooling systems each have both a source and a distribution system. The heat source will probably be a furnace powered by oil, gas, or electricity. The cooling system will typically use a refrigerant to cool air or a heat pump that removes heat from the air to make it cooler. The distribution system is usually built of hollow shafts or pipes in the floors, walls, and ceilings that carry the air to specific rooms. Some systems also have a return system that brings air back to the furnace or cooling system for reprocessing.

This overview of heating and cooling systems is offered to suggest that you will need to consider them as you plan your remodeling. In some cases, remodeling a home means upgrading or expanding one or both of these systems.

How Older Homes Were Built

Home construction is an evolution. New ideas and materials have been added from time to time, improving livability and efficiency. If your home is 20 years old or newer, home construction isn't a factor in your remodeling. However, older homes are constructed using older methods and materials that should be replaced or at least considered as you remodel.

Many older homes used dimensional lumber for framing, but typically of larger dimensions. That is, walls may be of 2 × 6 or even 2 × 8 or larger lumber. In some cases, the dimensions are actual rather than nominal; that is, a 2 × 6 piece of lumber is actually 6 inches wide by 2 inches thick compared to the modern or "dressed" size of about 5½ × 1½ inches. The *actual* size of your home's lumber is important to know as you rebuild and install walls.

In addition, remodeling a home means either maintaining the home's existing design or changing it to be more modern. In either case, you must consider what materials and techniques were used when the home was originally built.

Older Wiring Systems

Dig around in the attic or in the basement or crawl space under an older home and you will probably find a wiring system that doesn't look like those in modern homes. Early wiring systems used heavy-gauge wires wrapped in a fabric or rubberized coating. Some were simply bare wires that passed through wood via ceramic insulators.

In addition, the service box may use fuses rather than more modern circuit breakers. The total electrical current (amps) the system can distribute will probably be 100 or 120 amps, depending on the home's age.

What can you do about this? At the least, make sure that your home's electrical system can handle the extra load of electricity you need for your remodeling. For example, a kitchen remodel job with more lights, switches, and appliances will require more electricity, so find out if your system can handle it.

☞ **Money-$aving Tip #2** *Call an electrician to inspect your home before remodeling. Even if you're not adding electrical service, remodeling your home may give you a good opportunity to upgrade your electrical service. You can save money by planning smart.*

Older Plumbing Systems

Plumbing systems, too, have evolved in efficiency. Today's toilets, in addition to being more colorful, also take less water to flush than ones our grandparents used.

Consider how best to enhance your home's plumbing system as you remodel. You may simply use new plumbing fixtures and pipes in any additions. Or you may decide to replace existing plumbing pipes and fixtures as you remodel a kitchen or bath.

Some older homes were built with metal pipes that can be hazardous to your health. Testing your older home's water can tell you if it has excessive traces of lead, zinc, copper, aluminum, or other metals.

☞ **Money-$aving Tip #3** *If possible, plan to replace as much plumbing as possible with plastic pipes and safer fixtures. If, while testing, you also learn that your home's walls or ceilings have asbestos, consider having it removed by a licensed professional. The easiest and least costly time to do these replacements is while you're remodeling your home.*

Older Heating and Cooling Systems

As heating and cooling systems age, they become less efficient. In addition, the systems of today are more efficient than those of just a few years ago. So as you consider remodeling your home, also consider remodeling or upgrading your heating and/or cooling system at the same time.

In most cases, remodeling a heating or cooling system doesn't require replacing the distribution or ducting system. It usually means replacing the heat or cooling source. You may decide to replace an oil-burning furnace with a new, energy-efficient electrical furnace or one that runs on natural gas.

☞ **Money-$aving Tip #4** *If you're considering replacing an old furnace with a new energy-efficient unit, first ask local utility companies about your options. Some utilities will even help you purchase a more efficient unit.*

Reasons to Remodel a Home

The reasons to remodel your home are seemingly endless. The most popular is upgrading. That is, instead of moving to a new home you can upgrade the one you have to fit your expanding needs. Many families start with smaller, more affordable homes, enlarging as the need arises. Others enhance their home's livability without expansion. They simply upgrade.

Upgrading your home can be easily done as you live in it. An older bathroom is modernized. A bedroom is redecorated. A wall between the living room and family room is removed to combine them into a "great room." Newer siding is installed to improve the beauty and efficiency of the home.

Why you upgrade your home also depends on whether the home is one you've lived in for awhile or one that's newly purchased.

Changing Existing Homes

Families often grow, then shrink. Increased incomes usually allow for more amenities. A home-based business needs space. There are many reasons for changing an existing home into one that better fits your changing needs and lifestyle.

One of the advantages of changing the home you live in now is that you know it. It's familiar. You don't have to simultaneously change neighborhoods or even layout. All you change is what you don't like. Changing an existing home may mean remodeling your tired kitchen or adding a family room or expanding the attic. In each case, you're adding livability to what you already have.

One of the disadvantages is that it may be more difficult to remodel your existing home than to find another that has more of what you want.

Changing Newly Purchased Homes

Suppose you've purchased or intend to purchase a home that isn't quite what you want, but is close. You may be able to remodel it into what you want for less money than buying your ideal home. It may also allow you to upgrade your home on the installment program: kitchen this year, bathrooms next year, an extra bedroom the following year, etc.

Of course, to consider changing a newly purchased home, you must know what you want it to be like once you're done. This requires some planning. You may need the services of an architect, a remodeling contractor, or both. In some cases, you can include the proposed remodeling in your mortgage package and fund them together. (More about financing your remodeling in Chapter 3.) You can start your planning process today by watching for great ideas in magazines, clipping articles and photos, reading ads for remodelers, and even visiting builders' model homes for new ideas.

Understanding Remodeling

Thus far, we've been throwing the term "remodeling" around very loosely, as most people do. However, you should know the difference between *remodeling, renovation, repair,* and *maintenance* before you decide which one is right for your needs.

So, let's get out our handy-dandy dictionary and consider the terms of home remodeling.

Remodeling

Remodeling is the *functional* restoration of one or more housing systems. When built, the systems were modeled, therefore changing them is remodeling. The systems include structural (walls, floors, ceilings); plumbing; electrical; heating/cooling; etc. Remodeling changes or improves your home's functions. Remodeling modernizes both the function and appearance of the home.

Renovation

Renovation is slightly different. Renovation is the *historical* restoration of one or more housing systems. For example, a renovation of a kitchen returns it to the look, but maybe not the function, that the house had when new. Renovation restores. It may use modern plumbing and electrical components, but they will probably look like those available at the home's initial construction.

Repair

Repair is the functional restoration of a *component* within the home. For example, repairing a sink is neither a remodel nor a renovation. A repair simply makes the sink function as it did when new. A repair renews the function of the component, in this case the sink.

Maintenance

Maintenance is the *preventive replacement of components* within a home. Maintenance preserves the function of a component by replacing parts before they wear out. For example, maintenance to a floor means treating it with a wax or finish to minimize wear. It certainly isn't remodeling, renovation, or even repair. It is simply maintenance.

The point to these definitions is that remodeling changes the *function* of your home.

Considering Reasons to Remodel

Why should you consider changing the function of your home? There are probably as many reasons as there are homes. However, the reasons to remodel can be categorized into three broad groups. Your reasons will fall into one or more of them, but probably be in one group more than another. Defining the reason for your remodel will help you set your remodeling goal and ensure that you reach it efficiently.

Increasing Living Space

One of the most popular reasons for remodeling a home is to increase the living space within it. The space may be needed for additional family members (new children or aging parents) or additional functions (storage, business, hobbies).

Where does this new living space come from? It can be an unfinished attic that will be finished off into one or more rooms. It can be a basement that must now become a bedroom or other living area. It can be a garage that is remodeled into an extra bedroom or a heated work space. It can be one or more rooms added to the house. It can even be a second story added above the home or an attached garage. Where this space comes from depends on the layout of the home and property as well as the intended function of the new living space.

Improving Living Space

Another popular reason for remodeling is improving the living space you have. In this case, space isn't increased, it is enhanced. For example, a kitchen is modernized with new cabinets, plumbing, electrical service, and maybe even an upgraded floor. A skylight might be added. The size of the room is the same, but its livability is improved.

There are many projects you can plan to improve living space in your home. You can enhance a bathroom, make a closet into a more efficient storage area, refinish a dining room floor, install an ornate banister on stairs, add a solarium wall to the breakfast nook, install French doors to the patio, or enhance the lighting system throughout your home.

This book offers dozens of ideas for improving your home's living space.

Investment Opportunities

Remodeling can also be an investment. Some people buy, remodel, and profitably sell homes in their community, making a very good living doing so. Of course, they know which improvements are profitable and which are not. They also know what sells best in their area and how to find a diamond in the rough.

You don't have to be a professional homeowner to make a profit with your remodeling job. You can learn techniques from those that do, then apply those tips to your own home to increase the investment opportunities. This book will show you how.

Popular Remodeling Projects

You can probably see hundreds of projects around the home that can be considered remodeling to increase or improve living space. They involve any room or combination of rooms in the home from the basement to the attic.

Let's take a closer look at a few of the more popular remodeling projects: kitchen, bathroom, room addition, security, and disabilities. (The typical costs quoted are based on remodeling job estimating books.)

Kitchen Remodeling

Over 20 percent of remodeling projects involve the kitchen. They range from replacing the flooring to a complete replacement of all kitchen components.

Why remodel the kitchen? Even in the day of the microwave, the kitchen is one of the most important rooms in the house. It is here that people prepare and share food. It may be to simply add milk to boxed cereal or to reheat a meal, but it is still important.

For some families, the kitchen is where impromptu meetings are held to discuss the day or the morrow. For others, the kitchen is the room that offers the greatest efficiency in the home. If the living room is the head of the house, the kitchen is the stomach.

Which kitchen remodeling projects are most popular? Because of the change in cooking and eating habits in most homes—from stove to microwave and from dining room to TV trays—the kitchen has also changed. It is now the place where people go during commercial breaks. In those few minutes, a quick meal or snack can be prepared—or at least moved from the freezer to the microwave and started. So popular kitchen remodeling projects are often those that make the room more convenient and more attractive.

Leading the list of kitchen remodeling projects is changing cabinetry to hold a built-in microwave. Another is the installation or upgrading of a dishwasher and/or garbage disposal in an older home. Countertop replacement is also near the top of the remodeling list. So is cabinet replacement or refinishing.

Kitchen remodeling can be as expensive or as inexpensive as your budget allows. Adding shelving or replacing a flooring can cost less than $500. A full kitchen remodel with new cabinets and appliances can approach or surpass $10,000. Enhancing lighting can range from $200 to $1,000. Resurfacing existing cabinets and countertops will cost $1,000 to $4,000.

Bathroom Remodeling

In some households, remodeling a bathroom isn't a luxury—it's a necessity. This is especially true if everyone's day starts at about the same time. The door outside the room becomes the waiting room. People who later in the day love each other see each other as "the enemy who hogs the bathroom."

For other homes, the bathroom isn't ground zero for World War III. It's simply tired. It needs a major face lift with new flooring, fixtures, and lighting.

The most popular remodeling projects are those that add functions to an existing bathroom or add an additional bathroom to the home. For example, a 1½-bath home is upgraded to include a tub. Or a utility room is converted into a second or even third bathroom. Alternately, a new room added to the home is also built to include a bathroom.

Easier remodeling jobs include replacing a bathroom cabinet and sink or adding linen storage. Many people opt to replace a tired tub with a modern tub-and-shower combination.

How much will a bathroom remodeling job cost? That depends on whether you're adding a bathroom (requiring new plumbing and electrical systems) or simply upgrading the bathroom you have. A new bathroom can eat up $5,000 to $15,000 or more depending on how easy it is to add the room and needed utilities. Upgrading cabinets and fixtures can be done for $1,000 to $5,000. A shower unit can be installed above an existing tub for less than $500.

Room Addition

Room additions are the best remodeling option where space is at a premium. For example, many families who have new children or older parents to care for opt to add a room to their existing home rather than move to a larger home. Others purchase their home with an eye on how it can be remodeled later with a room addition.

The most popular room addition is the expansion of a short attic into a full or partial second story. In some cases, this is less expensive than building a new room adjacent to a first-floor room. In other cases, there isn't enough room on the first floor to extend the house.

How much will a room addition cost? The range can be from about $40 to $80 a square foot or more. So, a 10 × 12-foot room (120 square feet) can cost about $5,000 to $10,000. Much depends on what structural changes must be made to the existing home.

Security Remodeling

In this world of increasing crime, many people opt to remodel their homes for increased security. Besides the obvious—installing an alarm system—there are many things homeowners can do to remodel for increased security and safety.

Security remodeling projects include replacing existing doors with security or fire doors, moving windows to a minimum of 18 inches from entryways, installing quality lock sets, installing exterior security lighting, and building a *large* dog house.

The cost of security remodeling varies. However, it may be an investment, as some homeowner insurance policies offer discounts for security remodeling. Check with your agent.

ADA Remodeling

The Americans with Disabilities Act (ADA) increased the public's awareness of the number of people in this nation with disabilities. While the act doesn't affect private residences, it does make sense to consider "universal design" when remodeling your home.

Universal design simply means designing your home for access and use by anyone—short, tall, narrow, wide, or wheeled. Most of it is simply common sense. Minimize or eliminate steps and uneven floors where possible. Make kitchen countertops of multiple heights. Make doorways wider. Install curbless showers. You get the picture.

For more information on incorporating universal designs in your remodeling, contact the Center for Accessible Housing (800-647-6777) and your local building regulatory agency.

Steps to Successful Remodeling

Yes, you can remodel your home with ease if you plan ahead and take one step at a time. The home is often the largest investment a person or family will make. The decision to alter that investment by paying out more money isn't easy—but it can be worth it.

Whether you're remodeling to sell the home or just to make it more comfortable for the coming years, remodeling can be a good decision. It's one that requires planning and patience.

Remodeling professionals suggest the following ten--step program when considering any remodeling project.

Step 1: Assess your current situation. Do you have the funds, time, and patience to remodel your home? Does it make sense to remodel or simply move into a larger home? According to the American Homeowner Foundation, moving can be extremely expensive, typically involving a 6 percent commission on the sale of the current home, plus another 2 to 4 percent for closing, moving, and other costs. This organization suggests that if you like your present neighborhood, you should instead look into what improvements you could make for 8 to 10 percent of your current home's value before you seriously consider moving as an alternative to remodeling.

Step 2: Decide how long you intend to stay in your present home. Are you remodeling so you can sell faster or get a higher sale price? Or are you remodeling to create a more comfortable environment for a long-term situation? The answers to those questions will determine how much money you should spend and the scope of the remodeling project you should realistically undertake.

Step 3: Start defining the areas of the home that you want to change. You should have some idea of what the remodeling project will entail before you call a contractor. Cut pictures out of magazines. Make a list of rooms that need to be altered and the reasons for those changes. This information will help speed the design phase of your remodel.

Step 4: Clear plenty of time on your calendar for the project. It's unrealistic to attempt to remodel your entire kitchen the month before Thanksgiving! You should establish a realistic timetable with your contractor that allows for delays due to weather, supply shortages, or other glitches that may occur.

Step 5: Find a reputable contractor. The only way to protect yourself during a remodeling project is to hire a professional contractor. Make sure that you choose a contractor who is insured, licensed (if required in your state), and a member of a professional trade association.

Step 6: Create a budget. Decide how much you can realistically afford for the project before you start. If you are remodeling to sell, your budget should not exceed any projected increase in market value of the home that is the result of remodeling. If you plan on staying in the home for a lengthy amount of time, you should spend a little more to get what you want.

Step 7: Request a comprehensive proposal from your contractor. The proposal should tell you how much the project is going to cost and what types of products will be used. If the proposal comes in above your budget limit, talk to your contractor about other options. Sometimes you can accomplish the same look with other products or design techniques.

Step 8: Get a complete, written contract before the work begins. The contract should cover the description of the project, timetable, payment schedule, types of products, etc., with provisions for the responsibilities of the contractor, subcontractors, change order procedures, warranties, and alternative dispute settlement clauses.

Step 9: Tie payments to work stages. Be very wary of any contractor who wants a large amount of money up front. Normal contracts split payments by decreasing percentages of total cost and are tied to significant work stages in the project. Please note, however, that a large amount of money is usually required at the start of kitchen remodels to cover the costs of ordering appliances.

Step 10: Take a deep breath and keep your perspective. Remodeling can be noisy, time consuming, and disruptive to the normal home environment. It's important to keep your sense of humor and stay focused on the end result, not the process that takes you there.

Budgeting for Remodeling

You have a notebook full of ideas and a "wish" list for your home that includes everything you have ever dreamed for a home . . . you even know who has the skill to make it come true. Now all you need is to decide how to pay for it.

Financing can be a major source of stress in any remodeling project. Professional remodelers suggest the following options for establishing your budget:

- Keep the cost of your remodeling project in perspective. According to the American Homeowner Foundation, moving to a new home typically costs 8 to 10 percent of the current value of your home. This is a good base figure for establishing your remodeling budget.

  How much should you spend? The answer varies by circumstance. You should spend as much as is necessary to create your dream home if you are staying in the home for a long time and can afford to do so. However, if you are planning on moving, be sure to remodel within the standards for the homes in your particular neighborhood and a reasonable budget.

- Once you determine how much you can afford to spend on a remodeling job, *decrease* that amount by 10 to 20 percent. This money should be put in a reserve account to cover any change orders or incidental charges accrued along the way, which will prevent a frantic scramble for additional funds at the end of a project.

- Keep change orders to a minimum and remember that phrases like "while you are _____ , could you just _____" can quickly destroy your budget. Remember that any work not specified in the original contract will have a new and additional cost attached to it.

- You may want to obtain financing for your remodel, especially for larger projects. There are various financing plans readily available to homeowners. Among the most popular is the equity line of credit, which bases the loan amount on the equity in your home.

- Federal Housing Administration (FHA) loans specifically for home improvements are available through many banks and lending institutions. The FHA, however, requires that the contractor be approved by the lender; but be careful, it does not guarantee the contractor's work.

- Some institutions will allow you to borrow against the anticipated equity in your home once your remodeling project is complete. Check your local banks and lending institutions for more details about this form of financing.

☞ **Money-$aving Tip #5** *If you are buying a home that you intend to remodel soon, talk with your lender about including the remodeling budget in your mortgage package and fund them together to save loan fees. Also talk with your real estate agent about your remodeling plans and ask for advice and ideas.*

- A professional remodeling contractor or architect is familiar with many of the financing options available and can often help you arrange the financing you need. However, it is important for you to research various sources of funding to compare individual qualification guidelines, interest rates, terms, and tax considerations.
- Whichever financing plan you choose, stick to it. If you decide that your budget is "X" and your reserve fund is "Y," tell your contractor to work within those figures. It is easy to say, "A little more on this faucet won't matter. It's a small amount of money." Unfortunately, this is also an easy way to overextend your original, reasonable budget.

How *Your Remodeler Can Help*

Whether you hire a remodeler or do it yourself, ask the advice of a professional remodeler or architect who can usually offer you ideas and tips that will save you dollars and frustration. Many remodelers are members of professional associations (see Appendix for addresses and phone numbers of these organizations).

Architects have their own trade association: The American Institute of Architects (202-626-7300). You can hire an architect to design and manage the entire job or simply advise you.

Commonly Asked Questions

Q. Why did the previous owners use such ugly colors?

A. Tastes differ. One person may love a color that others hate. Trends also change tastes. Colors popular a decade ago when a home was last repainted may be "old-fashioned" today. Also, the paint the owner intended may look quite different once it is applied. Paint is one of the least expensive materials in remodeling, so choose one that better reflects your own tastes.

Q. How can I finish someone else's remodeling project?

A. That's a tough one. First, try to figure out (or ask) what the remodeling project was intended to do. Then make sure you agree with the intent before considering whether you want to finish it. It may be wiser for you to undo the remodeling project than to finish it. If you plan to finish it, list the steps and materials needed, make a budget, calculate the needed time, and tackle the project as you would your own.

Consider hiring a professional architect, remodeler, or home inspector to look at the job before you buy.

Q. How can I best inspect older homes?

A. By getting dirty! Wear coveralls, gloves, and a painter's hat to carefully inspect underneath, around, inside, and on top of a home you're intending to remodel or buy. Read the *CENTURY 21® Guide to Inspecting Your Home* for specific information on how to read the health of any home.

CHAPTER 2

Estimating Remodeling Costs and Benefits

Remodeling costs can easily get out of hand. The weekend remodeling job with a budget under $1,000 can quickly swell to a month-long project of $10,000 or more. Remodeling jobs that go beyond budget strain finances and relationships.

This chapter will help you calculate the actual costs of common remodeling projects in time and materials, then compare them with the equity and living benefits to make sure your projects are worthwhile.

Topics covered in the coming pages include how to calculate remodeling costs, estimating time and materials, adding equity in your home, considering living benefits, and how to make the best remodeling decision.

Planning for Success

Choosing the professional with whom you want to contract your remodeling work is only the first step toward a
successful remodeling project. You must also properly plan
the remodeling job.

No, this doesn't mean you need to develop a work schedule for the contractor or take final measurements for a new
addition, nor does it mean that you must manage every task
along the way. Your planning is what will give the contractor
a starting place to help you make your dreams come true.

Nor do you need to be a trained designer or interior dec-
orator to plan your project. But you do need to know what
things you like and don't like in home styles and elements.
The best way to start discovering these preferences is to
keep a notebook about what you do and don't like about
your home.

Be specific. If you don't like the cramped feeling of your
bathroom or you absolutely love the skylight in the master
bedroom, make a note of it. Start making a list of all items
you would want in your dream home. Perhaps that includes
a totally new kitchen with a center island or a master suite
bedroom with a fireplace and private library. Start clipping
pictures out of home improvement and decorating magazines. Jot down any ideas that occur to you along the way.

☞ **Money-$aving Tip #6** *The more time you spend on
deciding what you really want, the less money you'll spend
on things you really don't need.*

Once you have your wish list and ideas, start asking yourself some of the more practical questions required for a remodeling project:

- What features made us buy this house in the first place?
- What features do we ignore?

- What are the problems in this house that I would like to overcome by remodeling?
- Why do I want or need to remodel now?
- Is there unused space that could be changed to meet my needs without the expense of adding on?
- Are there other ways to accomplish my objectives, such as redecorating?

The more of your dreams and wishes that you can convey to your contractor, the better off you will be. Don't worry about organizing them into a single design. The professional you're hiring can sort out your various ideas and develop a cohesive style that works within your existing home while also working within the reality of your budget.

Careful planning at the beginning of your project will enable you to meet your needs and wants, update your home, increase the value of your investment, and customize your living space. It can typically do these things for a lot less than the cost of a new home and without the aggravation of moving to a new location.

Here are some additional tips from professional remodelers:

- Think your project through from start to finish. Your home probably represents your largest investment and its proper care and maintenance are essential.
- Look over your property carefully. What repairs are needed? What improvements would you like to make?
- Think ahead and determine your future needs. Do you need an additional bedroom, a refurbished bath, or a modern kitchen? Will you need a barrier-free environment in the near future?
- Review your homeowners insurance policy and make adjustments for the added value of the work being done.

Calculating Costs

You probably have a notebook full of remodeling ideas that include everything you have ever dreamed for a home. Now all you need is to decide how to pay for it.

Why Accurate Calculations Are Important

Imagine deciding to go on a long driving trip without first figuring out how much it will cost. You may get to your destination or you might get stuck somewhere along the way, broke. Instead, you know to calculate how much money is needed for fuel, motels, eating out, and some fun along the way. You will make sure that your calculations are current and accurate. If you calculate motel costs at $25 a night, you could soon run out of money as the reality of today's motel costs sets in.

You get the picture. Calculating the costs of a remodeling job must be done completely and accurately before you start the project.

Calculating costs is really easier than you might think.

Typical Remodeling Costs

Most people considering remodeling their home are stuck with some type of budget. There is a limit to what they can spend on remodeling. What is "typical"?

Of course, remodeling projects can range from a few hundred dollars to tens of thousands. As a guideline, consider spending no more than 10 percent of your home's current value on remodeling. This is a starting point, recalculated as you more closely define what you need and want to do.

For example, limit the remodeling of a $100,000 home to about $10,000. The initial limit for remodeling a $150,000 home should be around $15,000.

Special Remodeling Costs

Having placed a broad limit on typical remodeling costs, let's consider special costs. In some cases, the limit is too high. A home that is already overvalued may not be able to offer a good return on an investment of $10,000 or $15,000. On the other hand, investing in an undervalued home may offer a very good return.

Professional real estate agents agree that, unfortunately, many remodeling projects won't easily return your investment. These include structural projects such as foundation replacement and some room additions. Even so, they may make a good investment in the livability of your home and, thus, be worthwhile. Chapters 3, 6, and 7 will offer specific figures on remodeling investment opportunities.

The decision of whether to spend more than the 10 percent guideline depends on whether you plan to stay in your home for a while and let normal appreciation recoup your remodeling costs or whether you will move soon and lose some of the costs.

Estimating Time and Materials

So how much is this remodeling job really going to cost me?

That depends on many factors. The first step to answering this question is to closely define exactly what you plan to do. For example, a bathroom remodeling job may mean a new floor and cabinets or it could also include new tub, sink, toilet, lighting, and even a new window. Calculating costs means first defining the remodeling job.

As an example, turning an unfinished basement into a family room may require lighting, wiring, insulation, paneling, flooring, a new ceiling, and some furniture and fixtures. To calculate accurate costs, make a list of each component you'll need (two light fixtures, two light switches, 25 feet of wiring, etc.).

Next, take your list to a building materials retailer for an estimate. In fact, take it to a couple of retailers. As you do, ask for advice on how best to manage the remodeling project. Also ask for the names of remodeling contractors they would recommend. And, while you're at it, ask the retailer how you can establish an account with them. Some retailers will give you a discount of 5 percent or more if you buy over $1,000 in building materials from them.

Remodeling Time

As you estimate time and materials costs for your remodeling project, be sure to estimate the amount of time it will take to do the job and the inconvenience it may cause. Being without the primary bathroom for a month can be more than just an inconvenience!

Many do-it-yourself remodeling projects are tackled during vacation time. That is, the kitchen remodeling may require two weeks of full-time work on your part, leaving your trip to the Grand Canyon for another year. Or the remodeling may be done in stages, one weekend at a time.

Even if you use a remodeling contractor, you must still calculate the amount of time required to complete the project and estimate the inconvenience involved. A full-time contractor can complete a project faster than you can, minimizing inconvenience. Of course, make sure the contractor won't spread the project out over a long period.

The Added Costs of Part-Time Remodeling

Unfortunately, doing the job yourself doesn't always save you money over having a professional remodeler do the job. Tackling a large remodeling job on evenings and weekends will extend the time required to complete the task. This may not be a problem if you can work around the functional loss of the remodeled area. Doing without the storage attic for a few extra weeks, for example, isn't much of an inconvenience. But being without your kitchen for a few extra weeks can add many dining-out dollars to your remodeling budget.

Weigh the *functional* loss against the *financial* options to help you decide whether part-time remodeling is a good option for you.

Remodeling Materials

To help you in estimating remodeling materials, here's a proven rule-of-thumb: half of the budget will go for materials and half for labor. Of course, this rule doesn't fit all remodeling jobs, but it's a starting point. For example, remodeling a kitchen for $10,000 probably means about $5,000 in materials.

To more accurately calculate the costs of remodeling materials, you will need a complete materials list. You can begin developing this list once you've defined your remodeling job. Chapters 6 through 10 will help you develop your materials list. For now, use the basic materials list described earlier in this chapter. Make sure your list includes a description of each component, the quantity, the unit (feet, dozen, sheet, etc.), and the estimated price including any available discounts. Some building material retailers can prepare the list for you using your design and special computer programs, saving you lots of calculating.

Hidden Costs of Remodeling

It's what you don't know that can hurt you. Remodeling jobs often have hidden costs that only an experienced eye can uncover.

For example, adding a new room to the attic of a home may seem like a straightforward job. However, experience says that the existing foundation may need to be strengthened for the extra weight. The electrical service may need to be completely redone to handle the additional needs of the room. Changing the home's roof line may require that the entire roof be redone.

☞ **Money-Saving Tip #7** *Many remodeling contractors can save you more money than they cost. They know the hidden costs of remodeling. Get good advice so you can accurately calculate costs.*

Adding Equity in Your Home

One of the benefits of remodeling your home is financial. The improvements you make can often pay for themselves— and more—by increasing the value of your home. As mentioned earlier, the national averages for cost recouped within one year of completion are 104 percent for minor kitchen remodeling and 98 percent for a bathroom addition.

How do you know if the remodeling project will be profitable? By calculating the home's value *before* and *after* the project. We'll cover how to estimate current and new value, but first, let's discuss the types of valuation.

Types of Valuation

How much is your home worth? That depends on who is asking. For example, your home may be worth one figure to you, another to a prospective buyer, still another to your insurance company, and another to your mortgage lender. In addition, the tax collector will have yet another value on your home.

The market value of a home is the price that a buyer and seller will agree on in exchange for the home. Your home may be worth more—or less—to you. The market value also depends on what it would cost to find another home like it. You wouldn't sell your home for $100,000 if you know it will take $125,000 to find another home in the same area with the same amenities.

The insurance company wants to know replacement value or how much it would cost to *build* the home today. They may only pay you a percentage of the replacement value in case of total loss, but they still must calculate this cost. Of course, even if your home is destroyed, the land is still available for rebuilding so they don't figure land value into the equation.

Your mortgage lender wants to know the price the home would get under "distressed conditions"; that is, if they had to take it back and resell it in a poor market. This is typically about 75-80 percent of the home's market value. So why do some lenders loan up to 100 percent of a home's market value? Because you bought an insurance policy that covers the difference between the current and distressed market value of the home.

And then there's the tax collector. Taxes are paid on the *assessed value* of your home, which can range from 50 to 100 percent of the market value. The tax collector would prefer to base your taxes on 100 percent of the current market value, but it takes lots of work to figure and defend the market value. So most property tax assessments are based on a conservative market value that is periodically changed for all homes in an area, called a reassessment.

How to Estimate Current Value

So what's your home worth today? Of course, if you just bought your home you know its market value because a willing buyer and seller agreed on the value. Your equity in the home is simply the difference between its market value and the mortgage balance.

But what if you didn't buy your home recently? How can you estimate the home's current value? You can hire someone to appraise its value or you can do some research and calculations yourself. Remember that what you're looking for is the current *market* value rather than the replacement, mortgage, or assessed value of your home.

You can hire a real estate appraiser to estimate the current value of your home as well as calculate the value after improvements have been done. In fact, if you're working with a bank, you'll probably need such an appraisal to get financing.

☞ **Money-$aving Tip #8** *If your remodeling project is self-funded, you can calculate the current and new values of your home with some research. Ask the advice of your real estate agent for an estimate of market value. Visit the county courthouse for information on recent sales of comparable homes. You will be looking for the sale price of homes with and without the amenities you will be adding.*

How to Estimate New Value

Calculating the new value of your home after completion of your remodeling project is often more difficult without expert help. However, you can sometimes find an appraiser's handbook through larger public libraries and other resources. These handbooks can help you estimate the new value of your home with the added amenities.

The difference between the new value and the current value is the value of the remodeling project. For example, a $90,000 home that increases in value to $110,000 with an additional bedroom and bath offers a $20,000 increase. Whether this is a good investment depends on how much you must spend on the remodeling project. If less than $20,000, the investment is profitable.

Considering Living Benefits

Of course, not all profits are measured in cold, hard cash. There is great value in improving the livability of your home for yourself and members of your family. In some cases, you may decide to go ahead with a remodeling project even if the increase in financial value won't cover the expenses. In this case, you must consider and calculate the value of living benefits.

How can you estimate the value of increased space or livability? Let's consider this question for a moment.

Benefits of Increased Space

"It's my turn for the bathroom!"

Ever heard those words at your home? Or how about: "Where is grandma going to sleep?" Or: "The garage is too full to bring in the car!"

Most homes with growing families soon run out of space. Occasional yard sales help, but you may soon face the fact that you need more room. It may be a more efficient kitchen or more bathrooms or bedrooms. Or it could be that you need to install an office in your home. Whatever the reason, the benefits of increased space must be weighed against the remodeling costs before you can decide whether any remodeling project is a good investment.

What benefits would you and your family enjoy if you had more space in your home?

Which areas of your home most need more space? How much?

Can you increase space without remodeling? Can you change the functions of existing rooms?

What would your lives be like with the increased space in your home?

Benefits of Increased Livability

To make a house into a home it must be livable. It must offer benefits to everyone who lives there or visits. For example, to be more livable a home may need a more modern kitchen. Or it may require updated bathroom fixtures or a clean-up sink in the utility room. To learn what will make your home more livable, ask these questions of all those who live in it:

- If you could change three things in this home to make it more livable, what would they be?
- What do you like most about this house? What do you like least?
- What features have you seen in other people's homes that you would bring to this one if you could?
- Are you willing to give up our vacation time and money to make this home more livable?

Deciding to Remodel

Well, what do you think? Should you remodel your home or shouldn't you? Still haven't decided? That's quite understandable, as this is a major decision in your life, both financially and emotionally.

To make the decision somewhat easier, let's consider the best way to make the right decision. Let's look at the decision process.

The Decision Process

We all make so many decisions each day that the process of making many decisions often becomes a habit instead. To

make good decisions—especially when money is involved—
we must gather accurate facts, weigh each factor, get good
advice or counsel, then make a choice. The choice still may
not be perfect. In fact, it may require many compromises. It
may prove not to be the "right" choice. It will simply be the
best one under the circumstances.

Gathering Accurate Facts

Throughout this chapter, we've been gathering accurate
facts about your remodeling job: calculating costs, estimating time and materials, adding equity to your home, and considering living benefits. A critical part of this research is
making sure that the facts you gather are really accurate, not
just approximate.

For example, one homeowner was told that adding a
room to her home would cost "about $35 a square foot." It
was accepted as a fact, but, she later found out, it wasn't
very accurate. The final cost of the room addition came to
$67.28 a square foot—92 percent over the estimated cost.
Instead of accepting this approximation, she should have
gathered—and given—more information. The cost overrun
was due in part because the contractor was offering an estimate based on a rough room while the homeowner wanted
a well-finished room.

☞ **Money-$aving Tip #9** *Make sure the facts you get
are as accurate as possible. Get a second and even third estimate, asking for an explanation of any discrepancies. Being a smart consumer can save you hundreds or even
thousands of dollars on your remodeling projects.*

Weighing Each Factor

The tree of knowledge goes like this: with work, data
becomes information, which is then processed into knowl-

edge. Combine knowledge with experience and you get the fruits of the tree of knowledge: wisdom.

To make a wise decision about remodeling, you'll need to collect lots of data, transform it into information, then process the information into knowledge. Alternately, you can hire someone who is knowledgeable and trustworthy.

The point here is to learn as much as you can from facts (data and knowledge) and other people's experience (knowledge and wisdom) to make the best decision about remodeling or any other topic.

Getting Good Counsel

The importance of good counsel or good advice can't be stressed enough. If you hire a remodeling contractor (see Chapter 5), you will be paying for good counsel—or at least you hope you will.

How can you know if you're getting good advice on your remodeling projects?

First, ask around. Get some "instant wisdom" from friends and neighbors who have remodeled or had remodeling done recently. Who did they use as contractors and suppliers? Would they use them again? What would they do differently?

Second, test the counsel. If you've found a building materials supplier or a remodeling contractor you are considering using, start with a small project. For example, if you're considering remodeling the kitchen, use a contractor or supplier to redo a floor or tackle some other job to make sure your decision to use them is wise.

How to Make the Best Decision

Perfection is something no one or no thing on earth reaches. Don't expect it of yourself or others and you won't be disappointed. That's especially true of most decisions in your life, including whether or not to remodel. It's important, but it isn't REALLY important.

So gather accurate facts, weigh each factor and its benefits, learn from the good counsel of others, and make a decision. The decision may be "yes" or "no" or "not quite yet" or even "yes, however. . . ."

Doubts about a decision made often mean you didn't take the time to get the facts and counsel you needed.

Remodeling Alternatives

What do you do when there is no room to expand the home, but you need more livable space and storage room? You lie, cheat, and steal! That is, you lie to the eyes by creating optical illusions that draw attention away from the suffocating walls. You cheat the senses into believing the room is open and spacious. You steal space wherever you can find it, even if you have to knock down walls or confiscate closets to get it. This is not the time for a nice-guy routine.

Small space design is no different from any other form of design: It takes imagination, thought, and skill. In many ways, it is a puzzle that requires a professional who knows where to find the hidden nooks and crannies, and one who can play with an open, light, and airy feel.

The most important element in any room is lighting. It can make a room more enjoyable, and yet it is one of the most overlooked elements in creating the style and feel for a room.

Decorators recommend adding light and natural elements to small spaces. Add skylights and windows wherever possible. Windows that extend to the floor can open a space and draw the outside elements in; if a deck extends outside beyond the window, even better. The trick is to make a room's occupants feel or look beyond the walls, beyond the elements that normally would make them feel trapped. That will make the space immediately feel bigger.

If you take walls out of the limelight through your use of color and light, you will be able to make them feel like an extension of the room rather than a focal point. Good designs take the visual impact of the entire room into consideration, not just its individual components. If the eye is distracted and caught by too many individual elements, the room will seem smaller. But, if you open it up, you will make it work as a whole, not a random grouping of parts. While a particular window or flooring may be spectacular on its own, a coordinated effort that ties together all the components will make the entire room stand out. It will also make the room feel more spacious.

Windows are another place to look for an alternative solution. They open the house to the outside and draw attention beyond the confines of the existing structure. They also add light, something most of us don't get enough of. When windows are not an option (say in an interior room), use lighting. Consider removing soffits and installing lights that will reflect off the ceiling. Vault the ceilings and add a skylight for additional height. And always use a combination of ambient, incandescent, and task lighting in all rooms for increased ambiance. Use mirrors to add the illusion of space.

Often the bathroom is the room that is most overlooked where lighting is concerned. It also happens to be one of the smallest rooms in the home that could most benefit from good lighting. Consider adding kick lighting under base cabinets to illuminate the floor for late-night visits. Install overhead lights over the commode and shower, and task lighting around any mirrors.

The more light a room has, the bigger it will feel. But don't go overboard—it is unlikely that you will be performing surgery in the home! Intense lighting will kill the open, spacious feel; but careful and varied lighting options can create intimate moods or useful work stations. Another option for opening the home is simply to remove walls. This is particularly true in older, more compartmentalized homes.

When it comes to small spaces and existing spaces, the trick is to lie, cheat, and steal your way to the illusion of expansive rooms. It is possible to design a small space without adding square footage, compromising detail, or losing storage.

How Your Remodeler Can Help

Remodeling contractors know that not everyone who calls them for a quote will eventually hire them. Some will hire a competitor, decide to do it themselves, or won't qualify for needed financing. However, most professional remodeling contractors are like you: honest and fair. Tell them that you are considering a specific remodeling task and that you haven't decided whether you should do it yourself or use a professional. Give the contractor a chance to earn your respect and your business by helping you gather accurate facts and weigh factors, offering good counsel, and guiding you in the decision process.

Commonly Asked Questions

Q. How long should a remodeling job take?

A. That depends on good planning and your available time. If you're willing to give up your vacation or pay for overtime, you can get your remodeling job done in a day or a week, depending on the task. Or you can fund it as you go, spending spare time on it. In any case, consider the costs of inconvenience as you must give up a part of your home while the remodeling is being done. Your building materials supplier can help you estimate the time required to complete most jobs.

Q. How can I get the greatest benefit in the shortest amount of time?

A. By carefully planning your remodeling job, you can sometimes get the greatest benefits from it faster than usual. For example, you can plan a kitchen remodeling project to immediately return the room's functionality (countertops, sink, appliances, etc.) in a day or two, then work on the cosmetics such as replacing door trim or counter splash guards.

Q. Should I remodel before selling my home?

A. That depends on the remodeling job. Many people prefer to tell potential buyers "this room was recently remodeled," while others feel the home will sell faster if they say "I've reduced the price by $1,000 to help cover the needed remodeling to this room. You can pick your own colors!" The best advice is: ask your real estate agent.

CHAPTER 3

Making Remodeling Pay for Itself

Remodeling can be an investment in both the equity and the livability of your home. It can give you more enjoyment from your living space today while offering more money for your home when you sell it.

Remodeling can pay for itself.

In this third chapter, we'll cover proven methods for increasing value of a home at the lowest cost. We'll discuss profitable remodeling, including projects that make your home more valuable. Then we'll cover specifics on the best ways to finance your remodeling and some options you may not have considered. Finally, this chapter will include some proven ways of increasing credit and reducing financing costs.

Popular Remodeling

One person's remodeling job is another person's eyesore. The garage converted into a family room may be exactly what you need to make your home more livable, but the next owner may rather have the garage back again.

How can you make sure that your remodeling project will be popular and profitable for you when you sell your home?

Think like a home*buyer*!

In the example of a garage-turned-family-room, adding a family room will expand your market of potential buyers but eliminating the garage will shrink that market. Consider, instead, adding a new room to your home for the family room—or adding a garage to replace the one converted to a family room.

If your remodeling job includes a wheelchair access ramp for the entryway, consider making it one that can be removed if not needed by the next owner.

Think like a homebuyer to make sure your remodeling project will be popular with all future owners.

Projects That Make Your Home Better

Dozens of remodeling projects can make your home a better place to live and more popular with homebuyers. They include replacing kitchen cabinets and flooring, upgrading kitchen appliances and fixtures, upgrading bathroom cabinets and fixtures, adding a bedroom or bathroom, adding a family room or den, adding an office, expanding the garage, adding a patio or deck, and improving yard landscaping.

Projects that make your home better are those that increase livability for you, your family, and future buyers. They are projects that increase efficiency, improve functionality, or enhance beauty.

Sometimes, as we live in a house for many years, we can miss seeing opportunities for improving our home that may be obvious to visitors. We no longer notice the unfinished kitchen or the crowded bathroom. To overcome this situation, use your return from a trip (or even take a vacation) to look at your home with new eyes. Walk into your home as if you were seeing it for the first time. If such a trip isn't practical, increase the lighting in your home for a day to help you see your home "in a new light." It works.

On the other hand, what you see as a sore thumb may simply be so because you're staring at it all of the time. For example, a bathroom that seems dull and needing remodeling may simply need to be uncluttered or painted. Or, instead of a full remodeling, you may be able to simply replace a damaged sink or faucet to make the room better.

Profitable Remodeling

Many homeowners consider their house more than a place to live. They think of it as an investment. They know that money invested in their home will earn a good return and so they put as much money in it as they can—as long as they know that the investment will be profitable.

What remodeling is most profitable? Because homes are typically priced by the number and size of rooms, projects that add to the dimensions and functions of a home are those that are potentially most profitable for the homeowner.

Projects That Make Your Home More Valuable

Many remodeling projects can add to the size of your home and, thus, to its value. These include both room additions and room conversions.

Room additions include adding a new room to the house— a bedroom, bathroom, family room, a second or expanded kitchen, a den, or office. The criteria is usually that the new space must be insulated, finished (drywall or paneling), and heated. Of course, if the new room is on the ground floor, it must have an adequate foundation under it. If on a higher floor, the home's foundation must be strong enough to support the added weight.

In some real estate markets, rooms can be finished off to make the home more valuable. At the time of construction, many homes' basements are left unfinished. That is, they aren't insulated, paneled, and heated. Therefore, they typically aren't counted as part of a home's living area. Finishing off the room can make it more livable and potentially more valuable. The same can be said for an unfinished garage. Smaller garages can be remodeled into living space or larger garages can be partially converted to add living space to the home.

Of course, make sure that your remodeling of an existing basement or garage meets local building codes. For example, basement bedrooms aren't safe unless they have windows above grade level large enough to use as exits. In addition, third-floor attic bedrooms must have additional fire exits.

And, of course, make sure you get the necessary building and remodeling permits from local building authorities before you tackle any remodeling job that changes the structure of your home.

The Value of Added Living Space

Besides the financial value of adding living space to your home, you may also profit from the use of the space. One popular remodeling project today is adding an office to the home. In some cases, the room is an extension of the home, while other houses require that the extra room be detached. Such an addition can not only be profitable as an investment in your home's value, it also can give you an opportunity to make some extra money at home.

Expanding a kitchen or bath adds livable value to your home as well. It may not bring in any extra cash, but it can help you reduce the money you spend on dining out or make getting to work on time easier.

Financing Remodeling

By now, you've probably come up with a good list of remodeling ideas that can enhance the value and livability of your home. Good for you.

But how are you going to pay for it?

That's what this next section is all about: where to find the money to remodel. It's a pretty important topic, as most homeowners don't have the cash on hand to tackle larger remodeling jobs. They must borrow. So now we'll cover where to borrow, how to borrow, and how to reduce the costs of borrowing.

Sources for Financing

Borrowing money is never easy. Fortunately, borrowing money to remodel is much easier than most types of consumer credit. This is because valuable equity in your home can be used as collateral for a loan. Equity, as you know, is the amount of money that would be left over if you sold your home and paid off the mortgage. For example, your equity in a $100,000 home with a $75,000 mortgage is $25,000. This equity is your collateral or the amount you pledge to the lender in case you default or don't pay off the loan.

What makes remodeling loans less risky for the lender is the fact that you're not spending the money on trips to Tahiti. You are investing the money in the home to increase its value to you and to the lender.

So what?

The less risk the lender has, the lower the interest rate! And that's good news for you, the borrower.

Where can you get this money for remodeling? Depending on the size of your project and whether it increases the value of your home, you can get an equity loan, a consumer loan, or use credit cards to finance your remodeling projects.

Equity Loans

As just mentioned, an equity loan uses your current or future equity in a home as collateral for the loan. If you increase your home's value by $20,000, you can probably get a loan for most or all of that amount to fund the remodeling project.

Let's discuss equity loans a little more. Most commercial banks and savings and loan associations offer loans secured by up to about 80 percent of the home's value. Loans of higher ratios are typically insured at an additional cost. By adding $20,000 in value to a $100,000 home, for example, the home is now worth $120,000. If the existing mortgage—called the first mortgage—is $75,000, the homeowner can probably qualify for a remodeling loan—a second mortgage—of up to $21,000 ($120,000 × .80 – $75,000). If the first mortgage is higher, the second mortgage will either be less than that maximum figure or will have to be insured.

Of course, much depends on the local real estate market, the current mortgage market, your credit, and other factors. If homes are steadily appreciating or increasing in value in your area, lenders will probably be more interested in loaning you money than if home values are stagnant or decreasing. In addition, banks are like any other business: at times, they actively seek to make loans and at other times they make few of them. Fortunately, in this competitive world, not all lenders have the same policies. The bank across the street may be ready and willing to offer great terms on an equity loan.

Consumer Loans

Banks and savings and loans aren't the only place you can get money to remodel your home. Thousands of other lenders are ready to lend money on your good credit rather than your equity in a home. Of course, the collateral for the loan is not as tangible—it's your word rather than your house—so they will probably charge you higher interest. But a consumer loan sometimes makes more sense for funding remodeling than an equity loan.

As an example, if you have already pledged most of your home's equity for the first mortgage, you don't have any left to pledge for the remodeling loan. To fund the remodeling project, you need a consumer loan.

Another example is that your remodeling project is too small to go through the longer process of getting an equity loan. So you simply borrow the needed money based on your good credit. This is a common method of funding remodeling projects of a few thousand dollars or less.

☞ **Money-$aving Tip #10** *Consumer loans are also a good option for remodeling in areas where home values are not rising. Short-term consumer loans can then be refinanced into long-term equity loans once the home's value increases.*

Credit Cards

Credit cards, as we all know, are the most expensive way to finance. The interest rate on most credit cards can be double that of equity or consumer loans. So why should you consider going the credit card route to fund remodeling?

Credit cards can be used to buy materials without paperwork or hassle. If you need a new bathroom cabinet and sink you simply go to the building materials retailer and put it on your card. Of course, if you don't pay the balance off during the grace period (typically less than a month), you start getting charged hefty interest.

☞ **Money-$aving Tip #11** *Ask if your building materials retailer offers a credit card or revolving charge card for purchases. Most can offer you credit at rates somewhat lower than what the major credit card companies charge. The credit application is typically short, requiring that you are currently employed, own your home, and have a major credit card. Some retailers offer their own credit cards with a grace (no interest) period of up to 90 days. Other retailers offer do-it-yourselfer's a contractor's discount—if you ask for it.*

The Financing Process

Wouldn't it be great if all you had to do was walk into the lender's office, ask for the money, and get it on the spot?

"Would you like that in $100s or $1,000s?"

In your dreams!

The process of getting money for your remodeling project can be long and sometimes frustrating. Some lenders make it easier and others make it more difficult than it needs to be. Fortunately, you probably have some choices and so can work with lenders that help simplify the process and help you feel like a valued customer rather than a beggar.

The steps in the financing process depend on the type of lender. Mortgage lenders have a process with more steps than a consumer lender or credit card company. However, as credit providers now share more information among themselves, this process is becoming easier for everybody.

The added step in getting a mortgage is the appraisal or estimate of value of the property. This requires that a professional appraiser check courthouse records, physically inspect the property, and estimate the home's mortgage value (a conservative market value) once the remodeling is completed. For this service you will pay an appraisal fee and a title insurance fee that covers the property's title.

For a more thorough explanation of the financing process, read the *CENTURY 21® Guide to Choosing Your Mortgage*.

Applications

The first step in the loan process is filling out the loan application for your selected lender. Most lenders use a similar loan application. You can get a copy from your lender and fill it out for yourself, making sure you have all facts accurate. Then make a copy and use it to more quickly complete the application form at the offices of one or more lenders.

What's on the application form? The usual: names, addresses, family, employment, what you own, who you owe, your monthly obligations, your great grandmother's cousin's maiden name.

Completing a rough draft of the application form will help you resolve any questions about your ability to repay the loan. For example, you can take your time and make sure that all of your assets (what you own) and liabilities (what you owe) are completely and accurately included on the application.

Fees and Points

You can be sure that there will be fees to pay with most types of loans. The fees may be small, or may be included in the amount being financed, but they will be there somewhere.

What types of fees? A new mortgage will typically include:

- Mortgage origination fee for taking and processing your application
- Credit report fee—pays the credit company for compiling and furnishing a report on your credit history

- Appraisal fee—pays the appraiser for setting a value for your property (not necessary with most consumer loans)
- Title insurance fee—covers any potential liens or lawsuits in case the ownership of your property is disputed
- Escrow or other fees for handling the taxes and insurance payments as well as other services

Because these fees can add a few hundred to a few thousand dollars to the cost of the loan, remember to shop around among lenders for the lowest *total* costs rather than just the lowest interest rates. There will be more on this topic later in this chapter.

Your Credit Report

Whether you finance your remodeling through an equity loan, consumer loan, or a new credit card, you will probably need a current credit report. The lender will order the report from one of the credit reporting services. By law, if you pay for the report, you are entitled to a copy. Even if you don't pay for the report, the lender must tell you how to obtain a copy from the reporting service. For a small fee, you can receive a copy and, at no cost to you, dispute any charges on your report that you believe are inaccurate.

What's included on a typical credit report? Most include identification (name, address, Social Security number, birthdate); your credit history (companies, account numbers, high credit, balance, and status); collection history (if turned over to a collection service); courthouse records (bankruptcies, judgments, and liens); and additional information (former employers and addresses).

If you request a copy of your credit report, make sure you get printed information on how to read your credit file. The report includes codes (such as J, PRM, R1, etc.) you'll need to make sense of the report. The document may also tell you how to respond to inaccurate credit reports.

Smart Financing Ideas

Now that you've seen how the financing process works, let's take a look at how to save time and money on financing your remodeling projects.

Every dollar you save on financing is at least another dollar you can invest in your home.

How to Fix Credit Problems

Let's say that you've been turned down for a loan to remodel your home or for a consumer loan or credit card. What can you do about it?

First, you can ask the lender to give you a copy of the credit report or the consumer telephone number of the reporting service. You can then challenge any credit history that you dispute. A bad credit rating can be someone else's that was mistakenly put on your report. Or it could be a bad credit rating on you that has since been cleared up but wasn't removed from your file. Some lenders will let you certify to them that a single bad credit rating is bogus, thus not holding up your new loan. Others will require that you clear the rating up with the service before continuing the loan process.

The best way to fix credit problems is *before* you make an application. That is, contact one of the credit reporting services and ask for a report on your credit. To be safe, get a credit report from two sources. There may be a small charge. Here are a couple of addresses:

Equifax Information Service Center
PO Box 740241
Atlanta, GA 39374

TRW Complimentary Credit Report
PO Box 2350
Chatsworth, CA 91313
800-392-1122

You can then contact the reporting service about disputed ratings. Knowing what your credit report says can also help you complete the loan application form more accurately.

How to Get Great Service from Your Lender

The lending process can seem cold and uncompromising. However, it's managed by people. As a borrower, you want to be treated like a real person with respect and trust. Offer the same to each potential lender, and you should get the same in return.

For example, start at the top of the organization, if you can, asking for the branch manager or loan manager. That person may not be the one who actually takes your application and walks it through the system, but that person can introduce you to the one who does—and help you if you have a dispute. Start at the top.

Work with friends if possible. That is, try your current bank and lenders before you contact other lenders. They will usually be more willing to lend to you than to a noncustomer. If there are some blotches on your credit history, your current bank will probably be more helpful to you. If their rates are higher than their competitors', you may be able to come back to your bank later and negotiate a comparable rate.

If there's a known or unknown credit problem, assume that it can be cleared up and that it doesn't reflect on who you are or on the lender. Be gracious and expect the same in return.

How to Find the Lowest-Cost Loan

How can you make sure you're paying the lowest costs for your remodeling loan? It's very difficult because some lenders don't want you to compare. Instead, they offer lower rates and increase them with extra loan origination fees, points, processing fees, and escalators. So how can you compare "apples with apples"?

The best question to ask is: How much will I be paying over the life of the loan, including all fees? Then, as long as the loan lengths are the same, you should be able to compare loans for the best total package.

Where this can get tricky is with adjustable rate mortgages (ARMs) that can change over the life of the loan. The only way to compare these loans is by using the same assumptions for all of them. Ask lending officers for the total of all loan and fee payments under typical conditions. These figures will help you decide between ARMs from a single lender, but won't be as easy to compare with someone else's ARMs. Why? Because one lender's "typical conditions" won't be the same as another's.

Another resource for mortgage loans is the real estate section of metropolitan newspapers. Many include a side-by-side comparison of current first and second mortgage rates including fees.

How to Reduce Loan Fees

"That's our policy" is an answer that many lenders give and many borrowers accept too easily. "Why are the fees on this loan higher than those of Crosstown Mortgage?" You can almost predict their answer: "That's our policy!"

So, next ask: "Who has the authority to change this policy?" This simple question can often bring you a reduced rate or reduced fees on your remodeling loan, especially if you're ready and willing to go visit a competitor.

☞ **Money-$aving Tip #12** *A reduction of ¼ percent on a $100,000 loan can save you $6,631 over the life of a 10 percent, 30-year loan. Loan terms are negotiable. You might save yourself a few thousand dollars by negotiating with your lender.*

How *Your Remodeler Can Help*

If you've selected a remodeling contractor to manage your job, remember that most have contacts within the lending industry. These contacts can sometimes save you time and money by reducing loan fees. In fact, many lenders require that major remodeling be done by a licensed contractor before they will approve the loan. Involve your remodeling contractor in the entire process to get your money's worth.

Commonly Asked Questions

Q. *What's the best source for a remodeling loan?*

A. The best source for a remodeling loan is the one that is least expensive in the long run. Look at the total cost of the loan before you select the one you may have to live with for decades.

Q. *How can I easily clean up my credit?*

A. Contact a credit reporting agency before you apply for a loan. By verifying your credit report, you can prepare yourself and your loan application for a positive response from the lender.

Q. *Why do lenders charge loan fees?*

A. Because they are a business and must make a profit in order to stay in business. Remember that successful lenders are those that offer competitive rates and fees. Ask your friends and neighbors if they can recommend a lender—or if they know any you should stay away from.

CHAPTER 4

Deciding How Much to Do Yourself

Are you really ready for this?

Remodeling your home can be quite a chore—or it can be fun. It's up to you.

This chapter will help you decide whether remodeling is work or fun or both. It will guide you in estimating your remodeling skills, how and where to expand them, and how to decide what remodeling you want to do yourself without ruining your pocketbook or your relationships.

Yes, relationships are a part of remodeling. Rumor has it that "remodeling" is grounds for divorce in many states. Friendships have been known to dissolve. Kids have run away from home. Remodeling your home has all the makings of ruined relationships: excess stress.

We'll fix that!

In this chapter, you'll learn to accurately estimate your remodeling skills, how to effectively increase your skills, how to plan for success, and how to cope with the physical and emotional costs.

Estimating Your Remodeling Skills

Know what you're getting into.

That's great advice for most any task, but it is especially useful advice for do-it-yourself remodelers. Understanding what knowledge you'll need, knowing something about the processes of home construction and remodeling, having a working knowledge of tools, materials, fasteners, and adhesives, and measuring your skills will help you decide whether to do it yourself or hire a professional.

Wait! Even if you've never done any of these jobs before, don't discount yourself as a klutz. You may be inexperienced, but that can be easily remedied. Many remodeling professionals offer their help to teach needed skills through books, videos, and classes. Others will show you how to do some of the job, then finish it up as needed. They save time and you save money.

Knowledge You Will Need

So what do you have to know to be a do-it-yourself remodeler? That depends on what you're doing. To paint and decorate, you may only need on-the-job-training in painting. Your paint store can help you select materials and even give you some basic instructions. Adding a new room to your home will be more complicated and require that you have—or hire—knowledge of home construction. Changing the function of an existing room means you'll need to know the basics of home remodeling.

Home Construction

Chapter 1 of this book offered an overview of how homes are constructed today as well as how they were built in the past. In addition, you can learn more about home construction through a variety of books available in larger libraries and book stores.

Home Remodeling

Remodeling requires more knowledge than how homes are built. You must also understand how they are efficiently changed. Later chapters of this book will offer specific knowledge on remodeling. You can also train yourself with books, magazines, and videos listed in the Appendix of this book.

Tools

What tools will you need and how should you use them? That depends!

The tools needed for specific remodeling jobs will be mentioned in the coming chapters as the projects are introduced and described. For now, consider what tools you've used in the past. Have you used a hammer, handsaw, power saw, paint brushes, rollers, wrenches, ladders, measuring tapes, electrical tools, plumbing tools, or other tools in the past? If so, what did you learn?

Take heart. Even if you've never used these tools, you can learn to use them correctly and sufficiently to tackle many remodeling jobs. You simply need to be patient with the tool and with yourself.

Cutting tools. Cutting tools include numerous types of handsaws, the crosscut saw, keyhole or compass saw for cutting wood, and the hacksaw for cutting metal.

The handsaw consists of a steel blade with a handle at one end. The blade of all-wood cutting saws is narrower at the end opposite the handle, called the point or toe. The end nearest the handle is the heel. Teeth along one edge are bent alternately to one side or other so that the kerf (the width of the cut) is wider than the thickness of the blade. This bending is called the "set" of the teeth. The number of teeth per inch, the size and shape of the teeth, and the amount of set depends on the use to be made of the saw and the material to be cut.

The crosscut handsaw is used for cutting across the grain of wood. It has eight or more points sharpened at a bevel like the ends of knife blades. A coarse-tooth crosscut saw is used for cutting green, unseasoned wood, while a fine-tooth cross-cut is used for more accurate cutting of dry, seasoned wood.

The ripsaw is designed for cutting with the grain of the wood. Ripsaw teeth, unlike those of the crosscut saw, are sharpened straight across the front edge and work like two rows of chisels.

The keyhole or compass saw is actually two saws of similar design and use. The keyhole saw blade is much narrower than that of the compass saw. The compass saw blade is designed for sawing curves. It has a wider kerf than the crosscut or ripsaw to allow for maneuvering. The keyhole and compass saws are available individually or within a set of nested saws, or saw blades that interchange on the same handle.

The miter saw is simply a short-blade handsaw within a frame that allows precision straight and miter or angle cuts.

Power cutting tools include the portable power or circular saw, the radial arm saw, table saw, saber saw, jigsaw, and band saw. The circular saw offers portability while sacrificing some accuracy. Circular saws are excellent for cutting decking lumber, but are not practical for most cabinet work. A good circular saw should have a 2-hp (horsepower) or larger motor, a minimum 7-inch blade (7¼-inch is most popular), be tiltable for bevel or miter cuts, and include a rip fence that guides the saw during long cuts.

The radial arm saw is a versatile shop tool that can be used for decks as well as indoor finish work. This saw allows you to place materials on a stationary table and draw the moving saw blade across it for greater accuracy. The saw can be rotated and angled to make numerous types of cuts. A good radial saw will have a 10-inch blade and offer at least a 2½-hp engine.

The table saw or bench saw is similar to the radial arm saw except that it cuts the work from below rather than above. The table saw is a better choice when sheets of plywood or other large materials must be cut. Common blade size is 10 inches and power is 1½ hp or better.

The power saber saw or portable jigsaw is a hand-held saw that can make intricate cuts. The short blade is inserted into the work, starting at the edge or at a drilled hole, and makes high-speed, up-and-down sawing motions ⅝ to 1 inch long. Decorative trim and circles can be made with the saber saw.

The jigsaw is the stationary version of the saber saw. It uses a small crankshaft to transfer motor rotation to an up-and-down cutting motion. Size is measured from the blade to the inside rear of the cutting area, typically from 18 to 24 inches.

The band saw cuts wood in a somewhat different fashion. It rotates a continuous thin wire-like blade mounted on rotating wheels. The band saw size is measure by the throat depth or distance between the blade and the rear post. Popular sizes are 10, 12, and 14 inches. The thickness of the stock you can cut is limited by the distance from the saw table to the top of the exposed blade, often 6 inches. Small band saws use blade widths up to ⅜-inch while larger ones accommodate blades of ½- or even ¾-inch. The wider the blade the less likely it is to break, but the less precise the cut it can make.

Fastening tools. The function of a fastening tool is to install a fastener—nails, screws, bolts, hardware, adhesives. Fastening tools used in deck construction include hammers, wrenches, nutdrivers, and screwdrivers.

The most popular hammer is the carpenter's curved-claw nail hammer. It's steel-headed, wood- or steel-handled, and is used for driving nails, wedges, and dowels. The claw at one end of the head is a two-pronged arch used to pull nails out of wood. The other parts of the head are the eye and the face. A flat-faced or plane face hammer is easier for beginners to use, but more difficult to drive a nail flush to the work surface. Experienced deck builders prefer a convex or bell-faced hammer because it allows the nail to be driven flush.

Wrenches fasten nuts and pipe fittings. The most popular all-around wrench is the adjustable-end wrench. Because its jaws are set at a 22½-degree angle to the handle, it can easily reach most nuts. Wrench handle length is directly proportioned to how wide the adjustable head can open. Use a 6-inch (handle) wrench to accommodate a nut (or pipe) size up to ¾-inch wide, and a 10-inch wrench for a 1⅛-inch nut. The limitation to adjustable wrenches is that the adjustment may slip during use and damage the nut.

Open-end wrench sizes are determined by the opening, not the handle length. Use a ⅜-inch open-end wrench on a ⅜-inch nut. The length determines the leverage. Box wrenches are closed-end wrenches, often with 12 notches that better grip the nut to make use easier.

The socket wrench is actually a two-piece tool. The socket holds the nut while the handle allows you to turn the socket. A ratchet handle lets you turn the socket in short strokes. A speed handle works like a wood brace, turning the socket by rotating the handle in a circle. Leverage can be developed to tighten or loosen difficult nuts using as hinged offset handle or a sliding offset handle. Nutdrivers are screwdriver-handled socket wrenches useful for installing smaller nuts that don't require high torque.

Screwdrivers are designed to install screws. Because there are many types of screws, there are also numerous screwdriver designs. Screwdriver heads include standard, phillips, torx, and allen.

Prybars and nail pullers are especially useful to the back-yard do-it-yourselfer as they offer leverage for dismantling old structures, breaking concrete, removing siding, pulling nails, and other jobs of force.

Materials

You'll also need a working knowledge of remodeling materials. That's easy to get. There are hundreds of real experts in this field near you right now, all ready and eager to help. Not all are equally qualified to advise you, but once you've found a knowledgeable materials adviser you will be on your way to doing it yourself.

Where are these helpful folks? You guessed it: at your helpful building materials store. A growing number of large retail stores specialize in helping do-it-yourselfers select and use remodeling materials. They offer regular classes as well as individual advice and instruction on everything from selecting drywall materials to wiring an addition and installing a new lawn. Learn from them.

Adhesives and Fasteners

Materials are held together using fasteners (nails, screws, staples) and adhesives (hot glue, panel glue, etc.). What experience do you have with these products?

Adhesives. Most folks have used a hammer and screwdriver, but may not have experience with adhesives. They're really as easy to use as they look. Adhesives are simply placed between two materials then compressed to allow them to chemically bond. The variety of adhesives available is because of the variety of materials. There are adhesives for bonding wood-to-wood, wood-to-metal, metal-to-plastic, and anything-to-anything.

Fasteners. The most commonly used fastener is the nail or wire nail, so called because it is made from steel or aluminum wire. There are many types of nails, all of which are classified by use and form. The wire nail is round-shafted, straight, pointed, and varies in size, weight, head, type of point, and finish.

In terms of fastener holding power, nails provide the least, screws of comparable size more, and bolts provide the greatest amount.

Here are a few general rules to follow in using nails:

- A nail, whatever the type, should be at least three times as long as the thickness of the wood it is intended to hold. That is, two-thirds of the length of the nail is driven into the second piece for proper anchorage, while one-third anchors the initial piece.
- Nails should be driven at an angle slightly toward each other and should be carefully placed to provide the greatest holding power. Nails driven with the grain don't hold as well as nails driven across the grain.
- A few nails of proper type and size, properly placed and driven, will hold better than a great many driven close together.
- Common wire nails and box nails are the same except that the wire sizes are one or two numbers smaller for a given length of the box nail than they are for the common nail. The common wire nail is used for framing decks and large structures.
- The finishing nail is made from finer wire and has a smaller head than the common nail. It may be set below the surface of the wood and will leave only a small hole easily puttied over. It is typically used for finishing work such as to fasten decorative trim.

Nail sizes are designated by the use of the term penny, referring to the length of the nail. Penny is abbreviated by the letter d: an 8d is an 8-penny nail. The approximate number of nails per pound varies according to the type and size. The wire gauge varies according to type.

The corrugated fastener is similar in function to the wire nail. Corrugated fasteners are strips of corrugated steel with one edge sharpened so that they can be driven into wood. They are useful for joining the mitered corners of rail caps and for fastening similar nonstressed wood. Corrugated fasteners are available in a variety of sizes. Drive the fastener into the wood with a hammer and distribute the blows evenly along the entire width of the fastener.

There are many good reasons why screws are so popular for many remodeling projects. Most important is they have greater holding power than nails and many other fasteners.

Wood screws are designated by head style. The most common are flathead, ovalhead, and roundhead, in slotted and phillips heads. Slotted roundhead and phillips roundhead screws are driven so that the bottom of the head is firmly flush with the surface of the wood. The slot of the roundhead screw is left parallel with the grain of the wood.

Wood screws come in sizes varying from ¼ inch to 6 inches in length. Screws up to 1 inch in length increase by ⅛ inch; screws from 1 to 3 inches increase by ¼ inch; and screws from 3 to 6 inches increase by ½ inch. Each length is made in a number of shaft sizes specified by an arbitrary but relative number from 0 to 24.

Working with Wood

Wood is the universal building material. It's strong, durable, easy to shape, relatively inexpensive, and good looking. Examine a freshly cut tree stump and you'll see that the millions of small cells are arranged in rings around the pith or center of the tree. These rings indicate a difference in the rate of growth of the tree during the various seasons of the year. In spring a tree grows rapidly and builds up a thick layer of comparatively soft, large cells that appear in the cross-section as the light-colored rings.

Softwoods are those that have evergreen leaves or needles, also called conifers. They include cedar, cypress, fir, Douglas-fir, hemlock, pine, redwood, and spruce. Softwoods are the most common choice for decks and outdoor structures because of their low cost, ease of use, and permeability by preservatives and paint. Hardwoods are those from decid-uous or leaf-bearing trees such as ash, birch, beech, cherry, chestnut, elm, gum, hickory, mahogany, maple, and oak. Hardwoods are popular with furniture woodworkers.

Large lumber mills process logs into lumber with huge band or circular saws. After being sawed, lumber is dried be-fore it is useful for most projects. Air-drying takes many months, so most softwoods sold today are either kiln-dried or green (undried). Kiln-drying requires that the wood is stacked in a tight enclosure called a kiln and dried with heat supplied artificially for a few days to a few weeks. Lumber is considered dry enough for most uses when the moisture content has been reduced to about 12 to 15 percent.

Lumber sizes are somewhat misleading. The nominal cross-section dimensions of a piece of lumber, such as 2×4 or 1×6, are always larger than the actual or dressed dimen-sions. The reason is that dressed lumber is lumber that has been surfaced or planed smooth on four sides (called S4S). One-by ($1 \times$) lumber is called boards:

Nominal Size	Dressed Dimensions
1×6	$\frac{3}{4} \times 5\frac{1}{2}$
1×8	$\frac{3}{4} \times 7\frac{1}{4}$
1×10	$\frac{3}{4} \times 9\frac{1}{4}$

Two-by ($2 \times$) and Four-by ($4 \times$) lumber is called dimension lumber:

Nominal Size	Dressed Dimensions
2×2	$1\frac{1}{2} \times 1\frac{1}{2}$
2×4	$1\frac{1}{2} \times 3\frac{1}{2}$
2×6	$1\frac{1}{2} \times 5\frac{1}{2}$
2×8	$1\frac{1}{2} \times 7\frac{1}{4}$
2×10	$1\frac{1}{2} \times 9\frac{1}{4}$
2×12	$1\frac{1}{2} \times 11\frac{1}{4}$
4×4	$3\frac{1}{2} \times 3\frac{1}{2}$

☞ **Money-$aving Tip #13** *Remember that actual dimensions of the lumber you buy will be a bit less than their nominal size.*

Board measure is a method of measuring lumber in which the basic unit is an abstract volume 1-foot long by 1-foot wide by 1-inch thick, called a board foot. Board measure is calculated by nominal, not actual, dimensions of lumber. The easiest formula for figuring nominal board feet is:

$$\frac{\text{Thickness (inches)} \times \text{Width (inches)} \times \text{Length (feet)}}{12}$$

The answer is in board feet. Lumber is often priced in board feet. However, most building materials retailers and lumberyards also price lumber by the running foot for easier calculation. That is, a 2×4 by 8 feet is priced at eight times the running foot cost rather than as 5.333 board feet.

Lumber grading standards have been established to offer consistent quality of building materials. The primary grades are called Select (best) or Common (good), each subdivided in descending order of quality:

- Grade A lumber is Select lumber that is practically free of defects and blemishes.
- Grade B lumber is Select lumber that contains a few minor blemishes.
- Grade C lumber is Select lumber that contains more numerous and more significant blemishes than grade B. All of these flaws must be capable of being easily and thoroughly concealed with paint.
- Grade D lumber is Select lumber that contains more numerous and more significant blemishes than grade C, but is still capable of presenting a satisfactory appearance when painted.
- No. 1 Common lumber is sound, tight-knotted stock, containing only a few minor defects. It must be suitable for use as watertight lumber.

- No. 2 Common lumber contains a limited number of significant defects, but no knot holes or other serious defects. It must be suitable for use as grain-tight lumber.
- No. 3 Common lumber contains a few defects that are larger and coarser than those in No. 2 common; occasional knot holes, for example.
- No. 4 Common lumber is low-quality material, containing serious defects like knot holes, checks, shakes, and decay.
- No. 5 Common lumber is capable only of holding together under ordinary handling.

Some grading associations also use the grades of Construction, Standard, Utility, and Economy.

Plywood is made by gluing thin slices of wood together with the grain of one layer running at right angles to the other. This method makes plywood extremely strong for its comparatively thin size. Plywood can be sawed, nailed, and glued exactly like any other wood. It can be purchased in sheets of thicknesses from ⅛ inch, called veneer, to 1¹/₁₆ inches, as rough lumber core.

The term plywood grade may refer to panel grade or to veneer grade. Panel grades are generally identified in terms of the veneer grade used on the face and back of the panel, such as A-B or B-C, or by a name suggesting the panel's designed end use, such as sheathing or underlayment.

Veneer grades define veneer appearance in terms of natural unrepaired growth characteristics and allowable number and size of repairs that may be made during manufacture. The highest quality of veneer is A, the lowest D. The minimum grade of veneer permitted in exterior plywood is C.

Exterior panels have a fully waterproof bond and are designed for applications subject to continuous weather or to moisture.

Working with Plumbing

As stated earlier, the plumbing in your home is composed of two separate subsystems. One system brings fresh water in, and the other system takes wastewater out. If you and your family are to stay healthy, you must avoid any cross-connection between the supply and disposal lines.

The water that comes into your home is under pressure. It enters your home under enough pressure to allow it to travel upstairs, around corners, or wherever else it's needed.

Once the water has passed through the main supply line to your individual supply line, water meter, and main shut-off valve, it travels to the different fixtures in the house for your use. Water must be heated for your hot-water supply, but the water from the main supply is immediately ready for your cold-water needs.

The hot-water supply requires another step. One pipe carries water from the cold-water system to your water heater. From the heater, a hot-water line carries the heated water to all the fixtures, outlets, and appliances that require hot water. You can adjust the water temperature by raising or lowering the temperature setting on the water heater. A thermostat on the heater maintains the temperature you select by turning the device's heating elements on and off as required. The normal temperature setting for a home water heater is between 140° and 160° Fahrenheit, but 120°F is usually adequate, and is also more economical. Some automatic dishwashers require higher temperature water, though many of these have a water heater within them that boosts the temperature another 20°F.

Traps are vital components of the drainage system. You can see a trap under every sink or lavatory. It is the curved or S-shaped section of pipe under the drain. Water flows from the basin with enough force to go through the trap and on out through the drain pipe, but enough water stays in the trap to form a seal that prevents sewer gas from backing up into your home. If there were no seal at the drain, bad odors and dangerous gases would back up through the pipes.

Every fixture must have a trap. Toilets are self-trapped and don't require an additional trap at the drain. Bathtubs frequently have drum traps, which not only form a seal against sewer gas but also collect hair and dirt to prevent clogged drains. Some kitchen sinks have grease traps, which collect grease that goes down the sink drain that might otherwise cause clogging. Because grease and hair are generally the causes of drain clogs, traps often have clean-out plugs that give you easier access to remove or break up any clogs.

Working with Paints

Selecting the best paint for the job is important. Though there are paints for every possible surface, there is no such thing as an all-surface paint. Because the wrong paint can damage a wall surface and often not adhere well, it's crucial to know in advance what goes where and when. Fortunately, modern paint technology has taken a lot of risk out of choosing the best paint.

For safety, talk with your paint store professionals about removing any old paint, as some contains lead and requires special precautions for removal.

An important factor in paint selection is its gloss. High-gloss paints are the most durable because they have more resin than either semigloss or flat paints. Resin hardens as the paint dries. The more resin, the harder the surface. So, for kitchens, bathrooms, utility rooms, doors, windows, and trim, high-gloss paints are ideal. Semigloss paints, with less resin and a reduced surface shine are slightly less wear-resistant, but still suitable for most woodwork. Finally, flat paints are the coatings of choice for most interior walls and ceilings because they provide an attractive low-glare finish for surfaces that take little abuse and require only infrequent washings.

☞ **Money-Saving Tip #14** *Regardless of the type of paint you choose, its gloss is the most important factor because it affects both the paint's appearance and durability.*

Today, most latex paints are made with water as the thinner but with resins that are not latex rubber. Instead, acrylic latex paints contain a plastic resin made of acrylics or polyvinyls rather than rubber.

Why use an acrylic latex paint? In addition to the speed of drying and new opacity and washability of acrylic latex paints, the greatest advantage of water-thinnables is that you can clean up with water.

Latex paint works well on surfaces previously painted with latex or flat oil-base paints. It can even be used on unprimed drywall or unpainted masonry. However, latex usually does not adhere well to high-gloss finishes and, even though it can be used on wallpaper, there is a risk that the water in the paint may cause the paper to peel away from the wall. Because of its water content, latex will cause bare steel to rust and will raise the grain on raw wood.

The use of synthetic alkyd resin for solvent-thinned (oil-base) paints makes the paint yogurt-thick. A brush dipped in it carries many times as much paint to the surface as previous versions. Yet the paint spreads and smooths readily. The best way to clean equipment after painting depends on the type of paint you're using. Oil-based paints require a petroleum-based paint thinner; acrylic latex typically requires only water. As you buy paint, ask your retailer for tips on how best to clean up afterwards.

In most gloss and semigloss (or satin) paints, alkyd materials are still preferred for trim, doors, even heavy-traffic hallways. Many homeowners still like these best for bathrooms and kitchens as well.

Paintbrush protocols. The goal when using a paintbrush is to get as much paint to the wall (or ceiling) as possible without dribbling it all over the floor and yourself in the process. It will only take you a few minutes to be able to gauge accurately how much paint your brush will hold along the way.

☞ **Money-$aving Tip #15** *Condition a new paint brush before use by dampening the bristles with water for latex paints (or appropriate thinner for other types of oil paints). Then remove the excess moisture by gently striking the metal band around the handle's base over the edge of your palm and into a sink or a pail.*

Never dip the brush more than about one-third the length of the bristles into the paint. If you do, the heel of the brush will gradually fill with paint and be difficult to clean. With the first dip, move the brush around in the paint to open the bristles and let the brush fill completely. It helps pick up a full load if you sort of jab the brush gently into the paint with each dip. With most latex paints, dip the brush and let the excess drip off for a few seconds before moving the brush to the surface. With thinner coatings, gently slap the brush against the inside of the paint can or lightly drag it across the inside edge of the lip to remove the excess.

Using a roller. Working with a roller is even easier. Even a novice painter can get the feel of it in just a few minutes. As with brushes, moisten the roller first in the appropriate thinner. Roll out the excess on a piece of scrap lumber, craft paper, or even paper grocery bags. Don't use newspapers as the roller may pick up the ink. Fill the well of the roller pan about half full and set the roller into the middle of the well. Now, lift the roller and roll it down the slope of the pan, stopping just short of the well. Do this two or three times to allow the paint to work into the roller. Then, dip the roller into the well once more and roll it on the slope until the pile on the roller is well saturated. If you've overloaded the roller, it will drip en route to the wall and have a tendency to slide and smear instead of roll across the surface.

The most effective way of painting with a roller is to paint a 2- or 3-square-foot area at a time. Roll the paint on in a zigzag pattern without lifting the roller from the wall, as if you're painting a large M, W, or a backward N. Then, still without lifting the roller, fill in the blanks of the letters with more horizontal or vertical zigzag strokes. Finish the area with light strokes that start in the unpainted area and roll into the paint. At the end of the stroke, raise the roller slowly so that it leaves no mark. Go to the next unpainted area and repeat the zigzag technique, ending it just below or next to the first painted patch. Finally, smooth the new application and blend it into the previously finished area.

Paint sprayers for really large jobs. For larger painting jobs, an airless sprayer is the most efficient way to apply paint. An airless sprayer uses an electrically run hydraulic pump to move paint from a bucket or container, through a tube, into a high-pressure hose, to a spray gun, and, finally, to the surface. Once you get the knack of them, airless sprayers are easy to use, but if you rent one, make sure you get a set of written instructions at the same time.

Before using a paint sprayer, mask off everything you *don't* want to paint. Tape drop cloths to every floor surface. Drape windows, the fireplace, and doors. Remove all hardware or cover it with masking tape. Mask switches and outlets. Paint from a sprayer settles a fine mist of overspray on nearby surfaces.

Hold the spray gun a constant 6 to 12 inches from the surface and maintain this distance with each pass of the gun. Keep the gun precisely parallel to the wall. Paint about a 3-foot horizontal strip at one time, release the trigger, drop down to paint another strip of the same length, overlapping the first strip by one-third to one-half. Next, go back to the top and start another 3-foot section adjacent to the first, overlapping the edge of the first painted area by several inches as you work your way down the wall again.

Working with Electricity

Your home's plumbing and electrical systems may seem quite different, but there are many parallels. Water enters your home through a pipe, under pressure. When you turn on a tap, the water flows at a certain rate (gallons per minute). Electricity enters your home through metal wires, also under pressure measured in volts. When you turn on an electrical device, the electricity flows at a certain rate, measured in amperes, or amps.

Electricity is delivered to your home through wires from the electric company's system. The electricity passes from the meter to the service equipment through three wires that supply AC, or alternating current. This three-wire system gives you 110- to 120-volt power for lighting, outlets, and small appliances, as well as 220- to 240-volt power for air-conditioning, an electric range, a clothes dryer, a water heater, and, in some homes, electric heating.

From the fuses or circuit breakers, circuits go to all the devices in your home. Feeder circuits use heavy cables that travel from the main entrance panel to other, smaller distribution panels called subpanels or load centers. All of the circuits that run from either the main entrance panel or other, smaller panels are branch circuits.

The 110- to 120-volt branch circuits go through fuses or circuit breakers, which are labeled either 15 amperes or 20 amperes. The 15-amp branches go to ceiling lamps and wall outlets. The larger 20-amp branch circuits go to outlets in the kitchen, dining, and laundry areas where heavy-duty appliances are used. Every home should have at least two 20-amp circuits.

A 15-amp circuit can handle a total of 1,800 watts, and a 20-amp circuit a total of 2,400 watts. But these figures represent circuits that are fully loaded. In practice, limit the load on a 15-amp circuit to no more than 1,440 watts, and the load on a 20-amp line to no more than 1,920 watts. How can you know the load on a circuit? Add up the individual wattages for all lamps and appliances plugged into each circuit to make sure there's no overload anywhere in your home.

A word of caution: working with electrical systems requires knowledge of how they operate and how to work on them safely. If you choose to undertake such projects yourself, make sure that you turn off the appropriate circuit(s) at the electrical service box or, better yet, turn off the entire system before working on it. Check with your local electrical inspector for codes, etc. If you have *any* doubts at all, or are not experienced, hire an electrical contractor.

How to Increase Your Skills

So, do you have the knowledge and skills needed to remodel your home? If not, don't be discouraged. As noted earlier, there are many resources for developing your remodeling skills. They include books, tapes, magazines, self-training, and even hiring a teacher. Resources for remodelers are included in the Appendix of this book.

What most people learn as they remodel is that they can do more of it than they thought they could. Sure, it may take more time. But remodeling can be a learning experience with its own rewards.

Practicing on Smaller Projects

Many of the skills of remodeling, such as painting and nailing, can be easily self-taught. You can choose a smaller project and give it a try. You will not only discover new skills, you will also learn more about yourself and your attitudes toward doing it yourself.

For example, before deciding whether you want to add a room yourself, consider remodeling an existing room, especially one that requires moving a wall or adding a closet. If you plan to tackle some of your own electrical work (if local building codes allow), consider first replacing older outlets and switches with new ones.

Another option is to help someone else with these projects. You may find a neighbor or friend who is planning a do-it-yourself remodeling job and could use some help. This is an especially good idea if your skills and experience complement each other: one does rough construction while the other prefers finish work.

Hiring Remodeling Skills

Chapter 5 will offer you specific information on hiring a remodeling contractor. You can also do some of the work yourself and hire professionals with the remodeling skills you lack.

For example, one homeowner planned to remodel a kitchen with his own custom cabinets but lacked the skills to rewire the room. He hired an electrician. To save time, he also hired a flooring contractor to lay the new floor once the old cabinets were removed.

Where can you find these supplemental resources? Ask your friends and neighbors for referrals. Also check local telephone books for contractors in the specialty you need.

Calculating Nonfinancial Costs

Remodeling your home can be expensive not only financially, but also physically and emotionally. To make sure you're ready to take on remodeling—especially if you plan to do some or all of it yourself—make sure you first calculate the physical and emotional costs. Is it worth it?

The Physical Costs of Remodeling

Even if you're in good physical condition, remodeling can produce aches and pains. For example, painting soffits under your home's roof requires that you reach above your head to apply paint. This can be tough on arm and shoulder muscles and joints.

To minimize some of the physical costs, start working out a few weeks before you start the job. What exercises should you do? Those that you will be doing as you remodel, but don't do now. For example, to paint soffits, start a few weeks before the job stretching your arms above your head. Then progress to lifting small weights above your head and moving them in circles.

Another aspect of this topic is safety. Professional remodelers know how to work safely; you may not. Make sure you use safe equipment and install it properly to minimize physical costs of remodeling.

These words of advice don't mean you shouldn't try your own remodeling. Just consider *all* costs, including the physical ones.

☞ **Money-$aving Tip #16** *Start getting in shape now with exercises that simulate the type of work you'll be doing. Saving a few hundred dollars on a remodeling project isn't worth a hospital stay.*

The Emotional Costs of Remodeling

Remodeling is a stress-inducing experience. Taking your house apart and hoping you can get it back together in reasonable time is a real chore. That's why contractors earn their money: they know how to reduce stress.

The best stress reducer is good planning. That means not only making a list of the tasks needed, but realistically calculating the time needed. To further reduce stress, set a reasonable deadline for completing the job. Any later and you call in the contractor to finish the job.

Some jobs, such as painting the dining room, can be done leisurely in the evenings and on weekends. Others, such as remodeling the kitchen, should be planned for minimal downtime. How long can you live without the sink and dishwasher? These jobs should be planned for a vacation time or at least a long weekend with all components nearby.

Reevaluating Your Commitment

This chapter offered information and ideas on why you should—and should not—consider remodeling your home yourself. We've reviewed the typical tasks, systems, and costs.

The next step is yours. Based on what you want to accomplish and what it will cost, you can decide to do it yourself or hire someone. Before you decide, read the next chapter on hiring a remodeling contractor. Then you'll be ready to start your remodeling project.

Best wishes!

How *Your Remodeler Can Help*

Some remodeling contractors encourage homeowners to do some of the work themselves. Others would prefer that you're not even in the same city when the remodeling project starts. Most of them are somewhere in the middle. As you decide whether to do the work yourself or hire a contractor, interview remodeling contractors about their attitudes and experiences. A qualified contractor can offer you options that you may not have considered.

Commonly Asked Questions

Q. Can I help the remodeler and save some money?

A. Maybe. Some remodelers are more receptive to do-it-yourselfers than others. A few remodelers started in the trade by doing their own remodeling, enjoying it so much that they built it into a business. Others prefer to have all work done by their own employees and known subcontractors. Frankly, in some cases, helping the remodeler may actually cost you more in the long run. Much depends on what skills you have and how long it takes you to do the job.

Q. Do I need extra insurance to cover my remodeling workers?

A. Good question! Most professional contractors have their own insurance for worker's compensation, accidents, and related risks, but make sure you ask any contractors this question. If you simply hire someone yourself to do part or all of the work, you may be liable for any accidents. Your homeowner's policy may cover such circumstances so talk with your insurance agent about your remodeling plans.

Hiring a Remodeling Contractor

Hiring a remodeling contractor can be expensive. It can cost you a few hundred to a few thousand dollars to hire the skills and experience a professional remodeling contractor can offer.

But it can also be profitable. Hiring a knowledgeable and honest remodeling contractor can save you money in the long run.

The information in this chapter is gleaned from dozens of sources to help you make the best choices about hiring a remodeling contractor. First, we'll cover how to find, interview, and check out remodeling contractors. Then we'll consider how to efficiently select and use subcontractors. Hiring contractors and subs is next, followed by tips on how to work with contractors and solve problems.

This chapter can save you both money and stress as you learn how and whom to hire.

Finding Remodeling Contractors

A recent survey reported that 78.2 percent of the population has an "Uncle Joe" who is a remodeling contractor. Just kidding. But it may seem that way as you start looking for someone to help you remodel your home. "Yes, my Uncle Joe can do the job. I'll have him call you."

Uncle Joe may be well qualified to take on your remodeling job—or he may not. So how can you find the best remodeling contractor? Knowing where to look and what to look for is the first big step.

Where to Look

Most trades have one or more associations that work to improve the professional knowledge and image of their members. Some do so through certification programs while others are simply referral services.

A leading association for the remodeling trade is the National Association of the Remodeling Industry (NARI; see Appendix for contact information). NARI is a not-for-profit trade association with nearly 6,000 member companies nationwide, representing over 40,000 remodeling industry professionals. They are the largest group of remodeling contractors.

Other trade groups include the International Remodeling Contractors Association and the National Association of Home Builders—Remodelers Council.

Also contact your local office of the better business bureau (telephone book white pages) to ask if they have any complaints filed on specific contractors. Even if you must pay a fee for the report, it can save you lots of money and aggravation later—maybe even a lawsuit. (Note: the fact that no complaints are on file about a specific contractor is not proof of the contractor's competence.)

The first place to look for a qualified contractor is among friends and neighbors who have had remodeling done in the past few years. Your questions will probably produce both endorsements and horror stories about local remodeling contractors. Word-of-mouth advertising can be the best for good remodelers and worst enemy of those who don't treat their customers well.

Telephone Books

The yellow pages of your local and regional telephone books offer a wealth of information about a variety of businesses. Remodeling and related contractors are included, usually under the following headings:

- Contractors—Remodel & Repair
- Contractors—General
- Drywall Contractors
- Electric Contractors
- Foundation Contractors
- Heating Contractors
- Landscape Contractors
- Mason Contractors
- Painting Contractors
- Plumbing Contractors
- Roofing Contractors
- Siding Contractors

What to Look For

Okay. You've opened the telephone book up—or found some recent newspaper ads—and you want to figure out which contractors are most qualified. Here are some tips on what to look for:

- Membership in national, state, and regional trade associations
- Contractor license numbers (if required by your state)

- Specialties that fit your needs (kitchen, bath, add-ons, siding, etc.)
- Three important words: licensed, bonded, insured
- Experience ("20 years experience")
- "Residential" (rather than a contractor that specializes in commercial remodeling)
- "References available" (if not stated in ad, ask)
- "Free estimates" (you should not have to pay for a quotation)

Interviewing Remodeling Contractors

Once you've selected a half-dozen contractors that seem most qualified, the interviewing process begins. These interviews will simply be conversations with the contractors to verify that what you read or heard about them is really true. There's nothing more amusing (or annoying, depending on your mood) than calling a contractor that advertises himself as offering great client service and not even having your call returned.

Interested in some statistics about remodeling contractors? The average age of remodeling contractors is 45, says NARI. About half of them have college degrees, and another 25 percent have taken some college coursework. More than 90 percent of remodelers are male. The average remodeling firm completes 88 projects a year.

How to Interview

Where should you interview potential remodeling contractors? The first interview, designed to narrow down the field to two to four contractors, can be held on the telephone. Later interviews with the best candidates should be done at your home where the contractor can size up the project while you size up the contractor.

To start your interview, briefly state your remodeling project. For example, "We expect our third child in six months and need an additional bedroom added on to our 1,600-square-foot home"; or "We're retiring and want to remodel an extra bedroom and bath into a home office." Also, let the contractor know where you are in your selection process: "I've just started searching for a contractor and am looking for someone experienced with this type of remodeling."

What to Ask

Identifying your need will help the remodeling contractor know how to respond to you. Contractors know that some callers are dreamers, others are ready to hire a contractor this week, and still other are their competitors trying to compare pricing. By letting the contractor know what your project is and where you are in the selection process, he or she can answer your questions better.

What questions?

First, ask about licensing, experience, certification, trade association membership, and similar facts. You may find many of the answers to these questions in the contractor's ad or brochure. But by asking, you're verifying facts and finding out how well the contractor communicates with customers. A key to the success of your remodeling project is how well you and your contractor get along.

Second, ask open-ended questions that require longer answers. For example:

- Could you tell me about your most recent remodeling job like the one I described?
- If I were to call your last customer, what would he or she say about your service?
- How do you select your employees and subcontractors?
- How long have your employees and/or subcontractors worked for you?

- Have you placed any liens against customers' property in the last year and, if so, why?

Checking Out Remodeling Contractors

Many of the facts that contractors give you can easily be checked out with others. They include facts about licensing, insurance, bonding, and customers. If you don't know how to verify these facts, ask the contractor these questions:

- Who do I call at the state contractor licensing board to verify these facts?
- Who are your insurance and bonding agents, and may I call them to verify facts?
- Are you certified? By whom? How can I contact this group?

Licensing and Bonding Requirements

Licensing and bonding requirements for contractors vary from state to state. Check the state government listings in your telephone book to find out how to contact licensing boards for contractors.

Alternately, call or write to NARI for a copy of their annual "Summary of State Contractor Licensing Laws." There is a charge for this publication.

Certifications

Many trade associations offer certification for members who pass required tests and have a specific level of experience in the trade. NARI, for example, has three certifications: Certified Lead Carpenter (CLC); Certified Remodeler (CR); and Certified Remodeler Specialist (CRS).

Applicants for certification must be working full-time in the industry, have at least five years experience in the trade, submit a full record of experience, and complete a one-day written competency exam. They must also complete continuing education requirements to keep their certification active.

Using Subcontractors

Another option for remodeling your home is to serve as your own general contractor, hiring subcontractors such as plumbers and electricians, to do specific jobs. This can save you some money, but may not be allowed if you are financing through many lenders. They typically want an experienced general contractor or remodeling contractor to manage the job.

What Subcontractors Do

Subcontractors are specialized contractors who work in a single field. That is, plumbing contractors won't roof your home—nor should you want them to. They know a lot about plumbing, but may be no more experienced with roofing than you are.

Most remodeling contractors rely on subcontractors for work in some trades. A remodeling contractor who specializes in adding rooms on to homes may use subcontractors (subs) to do any plumbing or wiring.

Do-it-yourself homeowners may call on subcontractors to do a portion of the remodel that the homeowner doesn't have the time, skill, and/or tools to complete.

How to Find Subcontractors

You can find subcontractors the same way you search for remodeling contractors: ask friends, check the phone book, look for trade association membership and certification.

Remember that to hire subs, you should have a more in-depth knowledge of construction and remodeling than most

consumers. If you don't, hire a remodeling or general contractor to hire and manage subs.

Hiring Contractors and Subcontractors

How do you hire contractors and subcontractors? In writing! That is, don't depend on a verbal agreement to maintain
peace. In fact, if you're using a traditional lender, the bank
representative will require a written contract before approving the loan.

Writing a Contract

One of the most critical steps in any remodeling project is
the contract. This is the one item that holds the job together
and ensures that everyone involved agrees to the same
vision and scope for the project.

☞ **Money-$aving Tip #17** *Fully clarifying in the con-
tract what the contractor will and will not do regarding the
protection of your personal property in your home can
save you money for additional insurance or time for
cleanup after remodeling.*

Here are some key areas that homeowners should look for
before signing any contract:

- Be sure the contract includes the contractor's name,
  address, telephone, and license number (if applicable).
- The contract should include the approximate start
  date(s) and significant completion date(s).
- Detail what the contractor will and won't do, such as
  protection of your household goods surrounding the
  job site and daily cleanup or cleanup on completion of
  the job. Because this is an additional labor cost for the
  contractor, it may slightly raise the cost of the job but
  can be worth the price.

- Study all required plans (drawings, specs, and blueprints) carefully before approving them. Conditions to obtain the homeowner's approval should be included in the contract before work begins.
- The contract should include procedures for handling changes to the plans requested by the homeowner during construction—also known as change orders.
- Specify all materials. Your contractor should provide a detailed list of all materials for the project in your contract. This list should include product, size, color, model, brand name, and quantity.
- Explain all financial terms. Make sure that the terms are spelled out in the contract. The total price, payment schedule, and a cancellation policy (if there is one) should be clear.

☞ **Money-$aving Tip #18** *Make sure your remodeling contractor's subcontractors cannot file a lien on your property if they aren't paid by your contractor. How? Your attorney can include an appropriate clause in your contract, potentially saving you money and headaches.*

- Make sure any warranties offered are written into the contract. A warranty must be identified as either "full" or "limited." If it is a full warranty, all faulty products must be repaired or replaced, or your money is returned. A limited warranty indicates that all replacements and refunds of damaged products are limited or restricted in some way. The name and address of the party who will honor the warranty (contractor, distributor, or manufacturer) must be identified. Specify the time period covered by the warranty.
- Follow all building codes with any restrictions noted. Be sure that your contract clearly states any code or permit restrictions as well as any fees involved in the work being done on your home.

- Understand the entire contract before you sign it. Review the scope of the project and make sure that the contract includes all the items you have requested. If you don't see a requested item in the contract, ask about it. Otherwise, assume it is not included. Of course, never sign an incomplete contract. Be sure to keep the final document with *original* signatures.
- If the remodeling contract is signed at a home show, seminar, or somewhere other than the contractor's office or the homeowner's residence, federal law requires a "cooling off period." When signed, the contractor must give the homeowners written notice of their right to cancel the contract within three business days if they wish.

☞ **Money-$aving Tip #19** *Make sure that the contract with your remodeler includes the three-day cancellation clause required by federal law. If you change your mind in that time, you can get your deposit back without having to go to court.*

- A binding arbitration clause is also a good thing to include in your contract in case a disagreement occurs. Arbitration can enable both parties to resolve disputes more quickly and effectively without going to court.

Working with Your Contractors

Having a stranger in your home—no matter how pleasant or talented—can cause stress. Add that to the fact that this particular stranger will be swinging a hammer and making noise and a mess, and it's easy to understand why some homeowners consider remodeling to be stressful.

To help you survive, here are some tips to minimize the surprises and prepare you for a contractor in your home:

- Before work begins, ask your contractor what inconveniences may occur and plan accordingly for them.

Discuss the contractor's working conditions—estimated time subcontractors will begin work, mode of operation, etc. And do this before the work begins so you understand what to expect ahead of time.

- Clearly spell out any special considerations you may have; for example, asking that the workers not block the driveway without checking if the homeowner's car is out of the garage, etc. It is often these minor details that are overlooked in the planning stage and which lead to irritation later.

- Be sure that your contractor is fully aware of your vacations, business trips, or special events so that he or she can plan the work schedule accordingly.

- Move your personal property from the construction areas and declare all work zones off-limits to children and pets.

- Always put changes in writing if the scope and complexity of your remodeling project is modified while work is being done. All parties should agree on and sign any amendments before a new phase of the project is started.

- Keep a job file including the contract, plans, specifications, invoices, change orders, and all correspondence with the contractor for clarification should anyone question anything at a later date.

- Be open and honest from the beginning. Working relationships take time and trust. Discuss problems or irritations *as they occur* so you and your contractor can devise alternative solutions.

- Be patient. By the time you cook the first meal in your new kitchen or soak for the first time in your new whirlpool bath, you will have forgotten the noise, dust, and other distractions.

☞ **Money-$aving Tip #20** *Keep your mind on the end result. Getting in a hurry to finish a remodeling job can cost you overtime wages.*

Handling Contractor Problems

So what can you do if you're having problems with your remodeling contractor? That depends on the problem. For most issues, you can refer back to the contract to make sure its terms are being followed. Hopefully, you've made sure that the contract is a good one before you signed it.

Most remodeling problems between contractor and customer are resolved with communication. The best rule for good communication is: Don't take it personally and don't make it personal. That is, don't accuse your contractor of cheating you or let the contractor call you a liar. Instead, before words go this far, call in someone—such as your attorney—to make any required accusations.

But there's much you can do before problems ever start.

Watch for Problems

Looking back on most contract disputes, both parties can usually point to a single incident that started it all. Friends or relatives may have reported that "It started when the contractor showed up two days late and without his tools"; or "The contractor made a bunch of changes without asking, then wanted me to pay for them." So the best advice for handling contractor problems is to start watching for them.

Then what? Communicate! Remember: Don't make or take it personally. Just ask and tell: "I'm sorry that you weren't able to start the project on time. Our contract requires that I deduct $100 for every day of delay. My attorney would be angry at me if I didn't enforce that clause"; or,

"Our contract says that all changes must be approved by both of us or I don't have to pay for them. Sorry."

Define Problems Clearly to Solve Problems Quickly

As problems arise, the best way to get a quick solution is to make sure you understand the problem. That is, find out if the problem was caused by a supplier, a contractor's employee, the weather, or you. Sometimes, it's a ripple effect: "I'm concerned about the delay in the job that is evidently caused by the electrician not showing up when he was supposed to. This has kept the drywall contractor from being able to finish, and thus will delay my completion payment to you."

The problem—the late electrician—is clearly identified to the contractor. This is a much more effective way to communicate than simply saying, "You're late, so I'm not paying!"

With the problem defined, the contractor can quickly call in another electrician. Then the drywall contractor can get the crew in to finish up.

Don't make it personal, so it will stay solvable.

How Your Remodeler Can Help

Depending on the size and duration of your remodeling project, the contractor may or may not be on-site all the time. In fact, some contractors will only be there for the start and end of the project. If so, you'll have to be the contractor's eyes and ears. Let the contractor know of any potential problems: "The painter left at noon today without finishing the bathroom;" or "I know you want this job to be satisfactory to us, so please ask the electrician to clean up his work site tomorrow morning."

Commonly Asked Questions

Q. *What should I do if I have a problem with a contractor?*

A. First, communicate. Let the contractor know what the problem is and what you want done about it. Second, negotiate. If you're asking for something additional, offer to trade by removing a comparable part of the project—or expect to pay more. Third, delegate. If you're still having problems with the contractor, ask your attorney to call the contractor to work out a solution.

Q. *How can I help the remodeler do his or her job well?*

A. The best advice is: stay out of the way. Most remodeling contractors have experience working in houses that are also homes and will try to respect your privacy and living habits. However, you can really help by keeping children, pets, and other distractions away from the remodeling site. This may mean taking a few days' vacation or simply not using a part of the house for awhile.

Q. *What if the contractor doesn't finish the job?*

A. Before you sign your contract, be sure it covers this possibility. Most lenders withhold the final payment to the contractor until the remodeling project has been inspected and approved by an appraiser or at least the homeowner. Make sure that the final payment is sufficient to hire another contractor to complete the job if necessary.

CHAPTER 6

Remodeling Your Kitchen

The kitchen is one of the most important rooms of your home. It's not only where food is prepared, but also where people share themselves.

Yesterday's kitchen was simply a sink, an icebox, a small stove, and a cupboard cabinet. Today's kitchen often includes numerous major appliances, extensive storage, an island, a casual dining area, and maybe even a desk and an entertainment center. The kitchen is the heart of today's home. It is not only the cooking and eating center, it's the home's social center.

This chapter offers a number of popular ideas and projects for remodeling your home's kitchen into a beautiful and functional room. It includes step-by-step procedures for enhancing kitchen floors, walls and paint, cabinets, appliances, lighting and electricity.

Popular Kitchen Remodeling Projects

Families today have less time at home than any other generation to date. Most are living in two-income households, with children, and, in many cases, their live-in parents. The wage earners are the sandwiched Baby Boomers. And this trend toward multigenerational households is influencing modern kitchen design.

Today's kitchens need to be more adaptable and universally accessible. Multiple counter heights are becoming standard features, as are pull-out shelving in the cabinetry.

Experts agree that the keys to today's kitchen design are decoration, personalization, and customization. Homeowners want their individuality to show through with use of more decorative touches in the kitchen. Mullion doors, plywood end panels, mixture of wood tones, and multiple counter heights are all statements about the homeowner. The kitchen has become a room that is as consciously decorated as any other room in the home.

The kitchen is the center for new features and functions. Seating areas are being added, home office spaces are appearing, recycling centers are becoming standard, natural light is important, and the overall kitchen space will continue to open into the main living area through the great room design.

No longer is the cook relegated to the kitchen while the party remains clustered around the bar or rumpus room. The kitchen and family entertainment areas are now integrated. Today's kitchens are built for two or more cooks, and often include two work triangles, two sinks, and two preparation areas for double the efficiency.

Today's kitchens must meet the need for quicker, easier preparation of meals. Double ovens have been exchanged for one 30-inch oven with a second convection oven/microwave combination.

Technology is also in the kitchen. They have already introduced ovens you can turn on from your car phone. Other ovens have a control that you can lock before leaving the house for added safety around children.

The kitchen is truly the heart of the home, which is why kitchens are one of the most popular remodeling projects. It is a very personal space that is growing and pulling in outside elements. The windows are getting larger, the kitchen itself is getting larger, home offices are being brought in, as are computers, televisions, and family members.

The modern kitchen incorporates many elements, from flooring to the cabinetry to the appliances and countertops. All the major components and accent pieces must complement each other. Choose your star element and work around it.

Remodeling Kitchen Floors

Replacing your kitchen's floor can be one of the most productive remodeling projects. It can also be one of the easiest.

Flooring materials include linoleum, vinyl, ceramic, and wood. Flooring comes in sheets (linoleum and vinyl), squares (vinyl, ceramic, and wood), and strips (wood). In most cases, flooring is easy to install and will last 10 to 30 years or more.

Linoleum flooring is made of linseed oil, fillers, binders, and a felt backing. It is not as popular as it once was, having been replaced by vinyl. Today's vinyl floors are either hard or soft. Soft vinyl, sometimes known as resilient, has a hard surface and a cushioned underside. Most modern wood floors are made of either solid or laminate oak or maple. Many laminate wood floors use hardwoods for the top layer and softer woods for those underneath to reduce costs.

Here are the five steps for remodeling your kitchen floor.

Step 1: Prepare the old floor. Depending on what the new flooring material is, you must cover, remove, or at least roughen the old floor to accept adhesive. You can install *wood* floor over linoleum or vinyl flooring; however, installing *vinyl* over linoleum or vinyl may require additional preparation. The new vinyl floor will emphasize any imperfections in the old floor, so many remodelers first install a new "subfloor" of ³⁄₁₆-inch plywood. Others use a subfloor compound that can be troweled like cement to a flat surface.

Step 2: Measure the floor to find the center of the room. No room is perfectly square or rectangular. Starting the flooring in the center of the room minimizes any differences of width between one end of the room and the other.

Step 3: Start laying the flooring. To start tile or strip flooring, make a large cross at the center of the room and place the first four tiles at the *center* of the cross. To start sheet flooring, use the center of the room to align the design. Some flooring contractors use large sheets of paper to first make a pattern of the floor, then transfer the pattern to the flooring sheets in a larger room. The cut flooring sheet is then rolled up and moved to the new floor to be unraveled. Wood flooring strips are also started at the center of the room and installed, groove over tongue, and nailed through the tongue to hold the strip in place. Be careful not to damage the edge of the wood flooring as you nail it in place.

Step 4: Finish the edges. Whether flooring is in sheets, tiles, or strips, you will probably have some edging work to be done. You can cut sheet flooring with a flooring knife; ceramic or vinyl floor tiles with a knife, saw, or hard tile cutter; and wooden floor strips with a saw. You may first need to remove wood or plastic molding or edging.

Step 5: Clean up. Remove all excess materials, adhesives, fasteners, and dirt. Then clean and finish the flooring. Some flooring only requires mopping, while wood flooring will need a finish coat of stain and sealer.

For additional instructions on installing floors, read *Hardwood Floors* (2nd edition) or *Tile Floors* (2nd edition) both by Dan Ramsey (TAB/McGraw-Hill).

Remodeling Kitchen Walls

In most kitchens, the walls are covered by cabinets and appliances. The walls may show only about 12 to 18 inches of their height. The rest is blocked from view. But that doesn't mean the walls are unimportant. They must be totally functional as well as beautiful where they are exposed.

Kitchen walls are typically remodeled as the kitchen is remodeled. That is, the exposed wall surface above the counter is usually resurfaced as counters and cabinets are refinished or replaced.

Here are the six steps for remodeling your kitchen walls.

Step 1: Measure the height and width of the exposed wall surface in your kitchen. Remember to include the area behind movable appliances such as the refrigerator or free-standing stove.

Step 2: Consider how you will use your kitchen. If you'll do most of your food preparation on an island without walls, the exposed wall surface doesn't have to be as functional. A sturdy wallpaper or paint is probably okay. If you prepare foods on the main countertop near the walls, the exposed wall surface must withstand water and scrubbing. A hard ceramic or other surface is best.

Step 3: Select the most appropriate wall covering.
Look for a covering that will be functional as well as offer
the colors you want to use in your kitchen. Options include
plastic laminate (the same as used on the countertop),
sheets of copper or stainless steel, vinyl-coated wallpaper,
semigloss enamel paint, plastic masonry blocks, or cast marble. The measurements from Step 1 will indicate how much
material you will need.

Step 4: Prepare the wall surface. What this requires
depends on the existing surface and the material for the new
wall covering. Plastic laminate will need a clean, hard, dry
surface for adhesion. Stainless steel wall covering will need
little preparation. Vinyl-coated wallpaper will need the underlying surface to be clean and dry. Some remodelers install a thin (³⁄₁₆-inch) panel over the old surface for a clean
and smooth surface.

Step 5: Install the wall covering. Make sure that any
seams will fall where they show the least. Also make sure
that the pattern, if any, is level and aligned, especially for
long stretches of wall where errors can be most obvious.

Step 6: Complete the job. Trim as needed. Install edging and molding. Clean the surface following the manufacturer's recommendations.

Remodeling Kitchen Cabinets

Kitchen cabinets can set the tone for the entire room:
bright, subdued, modern, or classic. Selecting the cabinets
that best fit your kitchen depends on both your requirements and your preferences.

How much cabinet storage space should your kitchen
have? Many remodelers say that a three-bedroom home
should have 8 linear feet of countertop, 10 linear feet of base

cabinets, and 12 linear feet of wall cabinets. Recommended kitchen cabinets for a four-bedroom home are 9 feet of countertop, 10 feet of base cabinets, and 14 feet of wall cabinets. If you do much entertaining in your home, add another 4 to 6 linear feet of cabinets.

☞ **Money-$aving Tip #21** *Buying more materials than you need can be expensive. Use the number of bedrooms in your home as a general guideline and then adjust it up or down based on the size of your kitchen and your budget.*

☞ **Money-$aving Tip #22** *It is easier and less time consuming to install base and wall cabinets with their doors removed.*

The countertop in kitchens is the backdrop for the room. The countertop must blend in, but look good. It should be like a chameleon, blending in with the elements around it. But it is not the star of the room. Select the color of the countertop to accent the cabinets.

Here are the seven steps for remodeling your kitchen cabinets.

Step 1: Make sure that the floor is level. If not, you will need to place small pieces of wood, called shims, under the floor cabinets.

Step 2: Mark the location of studs in walls. Use a stud finder or tap the wall until you hear the solid sound of the studs behind the drywall. To test the location, hammer a finish nail partially into the wall to see if it hits a stud. You will be attaching the cabinets to the wall and into studs using wood screws.

Step 3: Place the base cabinets in position on the leveled floor. Check how the cabinets fit against the wall. If the wall isn't straight, install shims as needed. Then use a straight 2 × 4 to check whether the wall cabinets will need shims. Don't forget to leave the correct space to install appliances later.

Step 4: Install the base cabinets. Start with a corner unit, then attach adjoining cabinets to both the wall and other cabinets. Use C-clamps to keep adjoining cabinets together while you install screws at the back of the base cabinets.

Step 5: Install the wall cabinets. Place them at least 14 inches above the counter, depending on the height of the person(s) who will use the kitchen most. Screw the cabinets into the wall studs behind and the soffits above the cabinets. Make sure they are all aligned well before tightening down the screws.

Step 6: Install the countertops. You can purchase molded countertops or you can make your own with ¾-inch exterior plywood and plastic countertop material. Be careful: the adhesive needed to attach the plastic to the plywood is toxic. Alternately, you can install plywood and cover it with square-foot sheets of 1 × 1-inch ceramic tile and grout.

Step 7: Install cabinet doors and clean up well.

Remodeling Kitchen Doors and Windows

As you are remodeling your kitchen, consider remodeling the doors and windows into and out of the room. A new or enlarged window can add precious sunlight. A wider door can make the room seem more spacious.

On the other side of the remodeling coin, remember that a larger door or window not only makes more work, it cuts down on the wall space in your room. This is really important if your kitchen area is already too small to hold the cabinets you need. If you want more natural light, but don't want to cut back on cabinets, consider installing a skylight or expanding the room's lighting system.

Here are the six steps for remodeling kitchen doors and windows.

Step 1: Inspect the door or window opening. Measure its size. Decide whether you need to replace the door only, door with hinges, or door and frame. In the case of a window, inspect the unit to decide how easy it will be to replace. For both doors and windows, consider removing trim to inspect the frame that holds the unit in place. On older homes, you may find that the opening was modified by a previous owner and may already have alternate framing for another size.

Step 2: Select the replacement unit. Your building materials retailer can help if you have all the dimensions and a drawing or picture of the door or window.

Step 3: Remove the old unit. If you're replacing an exterior door or window, use a covering to protect the opening from the elements.

Step 4: Modify the opening as needed. In some cases, this means expanding or reframing the opening to fit the new unit. Make sure you insulate around the opening to minimize heat loss.

Step 5: Install the new unit. Following manufacturer's instructions, place the new unit in the opening, shim as needed, and fasten it to the frame. Make sure it is placed so that you can easily install the trim.

Step 6: Install the finish trim. If trim pieces need to be cut at an angle where they meet, use a miter box and saw to make the cut. Alternately, you can have your building materials retailer cut them to your specifications.

Remodeling Kitchen Appliances

Upgrading appliances is frequently a part of any kitchen remodeling job. You replace the old dishwasher or stove with a new one. You install a new built-in, side-by-side refrigerator to replace the old top-freezer unit.

So how and when you install new kitchen appliances depends on what appliances and models you select. Freestanding appliances are independent of cabinets. Built-ins depend on the cabinet for framing. A slide-in rests on the floor but the sides are unfinished and are covered by the cabinets. Most so-called built-in refrigerators are really slide-ins. Most modern dishwashers are slide-ins that have feet to help support their weight, but they are built into the cabinets with plumbing and wiring.

Make sure that you plan your kitchen appliances well. That is, if you're installing a new garbage disposal, make sure your new sink, cabinets, and plumbing are designed and installed to accept it. Also, make sure that your stove has not only a hooded vent, but also a vent pipe or duct to remove smoke and cooking odors from the room. Finally, make sure that your kitchen is electrically wired to handle the *combined* load of your new appliances.

Remodeling Kitchen Lighting and Electricity

Part of your kitchen remodeling project will be remodeling lighting and electricity. You will not only want to make sure you have adequate lighting for the expanded use of your beautiful kitchen, you will also want to know that you have sufficient electricity to safely plug in your power tools.

Fortunately, most modern kitchens already have sufficient electrical service to handle some expansion. And modern appliances that are more energy efficient than previous versions can give you more heating, cooling, and cleaning for your dollar and your watt.

Here are the five steps for remodeling kitchen lighting and electricity.

Step 1: Calculate your kitchen lighting and electricity requirements. Make sure your remodeling plan offers sufficient lighting in the areas needed most. Be sure major and small appliances have plugs and switches where they are most handy. A local lighting store or building materials retailer may offer expert advice for free—if you buy from them.

Step 2: Calculate the energy requirements. Electrical needs are measured in amperes, or amps. List and add up the amp requirements of all lighting and each appliance you will have in your new kitchen. If you don't know the amps, divide the watts (on the appliance label) by 115 volts. For example, a 700-watt microwave uses about 6 amps of electricity. If you have a 220-volt electric stove, it is probably on its own circuit and need not be counted with the other appliances.

☞ **Money-$aving Tip #23** *Save money by carefully planning electrical systems for efficiency. It can be very costly to get into a remodeling project and learn—after walls have been redone—that additional wiring is needed.*

Step 3: Calculate the available electricity. Your main electrical box, or a separate branch box for the kitchen, will show you how much electricity can go to the kitchen. Find all the circuit breakers or fuses that power the kitchen. If in doubt, plug a light into a kitchen outlet, turn it on, and see if it goes out when a circuit breaker or fuse is turned off. Next, add up the amperage of each breaker that serves the kitchen. Breakers and fuses will have a number on them, such as 10, 15, or 20 amps.

Step 4: Subtract the new kitchen's energy requirements from the available electricity, branch by branch. That is, make sure the electricity needs for one branch (through a *single* breaker or fuse) doesn't exceed the available electricity in the branch.

Step 5: Hire an electrician to make any needed changes in your house's wiring. Show the electrician your calculations and discuss options. Get a quote on any needed work. It will probably be easiest for the electrician to add a branch to the kitchen after the old cabinets are taken down and before the new ones go up.

Other Kitchen Remodeling Ideas

Of course, there are many other kitchen remodeling jobs you can tackle or hire to make this important room more efficient and comfortable. Here are just a few ideas:

- Add a skylight or indirect lighting module above the center of the kitchen.
- If space is sufficient, add a floor-to-ceiling pantry in the kitchen for handy storage.
- Consider adding spotlights to concentrate light on specific work areas in your kitchen.
- Paint your kitchen ceiling to match the colors in the floor.
- If you have or plan to have toddlers, consider installing child-proof latches to cabinets.

- Instead of installing new cabinets, consider refacing, painting, or staining the cabinets and replacing the countertops.
- Look for ways of using wasted space, such as installing a lazy susan turntable shelving system in a corner base cabinet.
- Make sure the distances between the refrigerator, sink, and stove are minimal for greatest efficiency.
- If your kitchen is too large, consider turning one end of it into a breakfast nook or snack bar.
- If you plan to live in your home for awhile, make sure the countertops and cabinet shelves fit those who live there, modifying your design for household members who are taller or shorter than "average."
- Remember that one of the best ways to remodel your kitchen on a budget is to improve the lighting and soften the colors.

How Your Remodeler Can Help

Your remodeler probably has many years of experience in the construction and remodeling trade. Use it to your advantage. Ask for ideas. Discuss problems you have with your kitchen and how to solve them at the least cost. Sometimes simply moving an appliance from one location to another can free up valuable space. Your remodeler has seen hundreds of kitchens. Pick his or her brain!

Commonly Asked Questions

Q. *What should I do about old asbestos linoleum?*

A. Many older homes have linoleum that uses an asbestos filler. As we've learned over the past decade, asbestos can be hazardous to your health. Check with local flooring supply stores and contractors to learn current requirements about replacement and disposal of asbestos linoleum. In some cases, only trained asbestos removal contractors can take it out. Your remodeling contractor can help.

Q. *Can I repaint my appliances to match my new kitchen?*

A. Certainly. There is a variety of paints and colors for refinishing older appliances. Make sure you know what the old finish is. Some finishes are plastic, others are metal. Some appliances have panels that you can easily remove and replace. The owner's manual on your appliance may be helpful. If not, contact major appliance retailers in your area. Some even sell the finishing materials.

Q. *What if I can't afford new kitchen cabinets?*

A. You can refinish them and replace doors and hardware at less than half the cost of new cabinets. You will need to remove the old finish or use a new finish that adheres to and covers the previous finish. Consider replacing the countertop because it gets more wear and can be purchased in preformed units through most building materials retailers.

CHAPTER 7

Remodeling Your Bathrooms

While kitchens may be where homeowners are bonding, baths are where they escape. That's why so many homeowners are remodeling their bathrooms.

You can, too. This chapter offers a number of smart ideas and easy projects for remodeling or updating your bathrooms in your spare time. It includes specific instructions on remodeling plumbing, cabinets, floors, decorating, and more.

Whether you do it yourself or hire a professional remodeler, knowing how to remodel your home's bathrooms is a valuable lesson.

Popular Bathroom Remodeling Projects

The biggest trend in bathrooms today is cocooning. Homeowners want to retreat from the world and their families. The American attitude toward the bath is changing. We used to look at the room as purely utilitarian. Now, we are approaching the bath as the Europeans do—we are seeing it as a place for personal pampering.

That may explain the rise in steam showers, rain bars, rain domes, double shower heads, body massagers and sprays, jetted tubs, oversized tubs, and in-line water heaters. Baths are becoming the one place to submerge problems and get away from life's stress and demands.

In a recent poll, 75 percent of consumers said that they wanted a larger master bath with a separate tub and shower. The poll also notes that 18 percent of all tubs are jetted and that the number is increasing.

Americans want to relax. Some are even going so far as to put their exercise equipment in the master bath to release their aggressions before climbing into a private sauna or hot bath. Not a good idea! Why? Because there is too much moisture in the bath for the health of the equipment. Putting it in the bath encourages rust and other deterioration. It is much better to create a separate but adjoining room for the home gym, experts say.

The trend for larger baths can be a trick when there is limited space to grow. If there isn't room for a separate tub and shower, experts suggest that you install just a shower. Don't try to combine the two. Why not? The tub and shower combination is difficult to get in and out of, reducing safety. In addition, a large shower stall with clear glass enclosure will increase the visual line of the space while still maintaining the need for a relaxing water experience.

Today, homeowners are looking at their baths as a form of water recreation. Some prefer a long bath in a tub with an in-line heater. Others want a shower with a rain bar. Other bath features include radiant floor heating, towel warmers, and steam showers.

Consider adding magnifying mirrors and enhanced lighting. Lighting is an important factor in any room, but particularly in the bath. Here is a room where you must be able to shave, put on makeup, find a fallen contact lens, sort laundry, and still be able to have a soothing bath or shower. Each activity requires different lighting techniques. Experts recommend cross-illumination: along the side of mirrors with an additional top lighting bar. The cross lighting from the sides will eliminate dark shadows. Use recessed cans and diffusers for increased mood lighting around the tub.

The other type of lighting to remember in the bath is natural lighting. Daylight is essential in the bath. Daylight not only helps people relax, it also increases the visual size of the room. Imagine, after a hard day, taking a long soak while watching the stars come out.

☞ **Money-$aving Tip #24** *Consider adding skylights, picture windows, and solar tubes to your bathroom design. They increase the light and open the view. Smart planning may reduce some of your electrical lighting costs.*

Another important consideration in designing your ideal bath is safety. As we all age, bathrooms become a dangerous place of slippery surfaces and difficult barriers, especially tub-and-shower combinations. Today's homes and baths need to incorporate universal design features such as higher vanities (30 to 35 inches), curbless showers, wider clearances around the tub and toilet, and easily manipulated faucets and hardware. Horizontal grab bars should be attached to wall studs.

Common bathroom designs include powder room (under 20 square feet), small family (under 50 square feet), medium family (50 to 60 square feet), master bath (over 60 square feet), zoned (with interior separating walls), adjoining, and dressing room (without tub or shower).

Lots of ideas for your remodeled bath! Select the ones that best fit your family's needs now and into the future. However, remember that a project to remodel the bathroom has the highest per-square-foot price in your home. Plan well, work smart, negotiate hard, and enjoy!

Remodeling Bathroom Plumbing

The bathroom revolves around its plumbing: toilet, sink, tub, and shower. So it makes sense that remodeling the bath often means changing the plumbing. In most cases, you won't be making many changes to the actual pipes that bring water in and take waste away. Instead, remodeling plumbing means replacing plumbing fixtures.

Alternately, remodeling bathroom plumbing may require that an entirely new bathroom or half-bath be added to the home. Where? That depends on where it is most needed as well as where plumbing services are now available. Many second or third bathrooms are added adjacent to an existing bathroom or utility room so that existing pipes can be tapped. That reduces costs.

In designing your bathroom plumbing, consider the following standards:

- The minimum size for a full bathroom (tub, toilet, sink) is 5 × 8 feet.
- Standard bath tubs are 54, 60, or 66 inches long.
- Standard height for shower heads is 66 inches for men and 60 inches for women.
- Standard towel bars are 18 inches wide for two face towels and 24 inches wide for two bath towels, installed 36 to 42 inches above the floor. Allow 27 inches of rod space per person.
- Sink cabinets are typically 34 to 36 inches high.

Here are the six steps for remodeling your bathroom plumbing.

Step 1: Design your new bathroom. Select the fixtures you want and where you will place them. Minimize the number of changes you must make to existing plumbing. Moving a toilet, for example, can add many hours and dollars to the job.

Step 2: Make sure you turn off the water to the bathroom before working on the plumbing. In many homes, this means turning off the main water supply valve near the water meter or water pump.

Step 3: Make structural changes first. Move walls, doors, and windows as needed before replacing plumbing fixtures. Also remove drywall or plaster as needed to access plumbing that needs to be changed.

Step 4: Install new fresh water and waste water lines as needed. Depending on how extensive your bathroom remodeling project is, you may decide to replace older cast iron or steel pipes and traps with plastic ones.

Step 5: Install new fixtures. Follow manufacturer's instructions for installing a new toilet, shower, bathtub, sinks, and other fixtures. Depending on what you're installing, you may need to install new cabinets or flooring before or after you install some fixtures.

Step 6: Finish the installation. Once a new tub or sink is in, install new faucets and related hardware.

Remodeling Bathroom Cabinets

For many homes, bathroom remodeling means replacing those old cabinets with new ones and adding a new sink and faucet. Some remodelers prefer to remove and refinish old cabinets, then install a new sink and top on otherwise structurally sound cabinets. Others add new bathroom cabinets once the new plumbing and fixtures are installed. In either case, remodeling bathroom cabinets is an easy task because of the wide availability of standard bathroom cabinets and vanities.

☞ **Money-$aving Tip #25** *To save money on your bathroom remodeling, consider installing a new sink and top on otherwise structurally sound cabinets that you refinish.*

If you do decide to replace your bathroom cabinets, here are the seven steps to follow.

Step 1: Plan your bathroom. Decide where you want your cabinets. If you are planning his-and-her vanity cabinets, consider including room underneath hers to allow for sitting down to apply makeup. If appropriate, make his 2 to 4 inches higher.

Step 2: Select the new cabinets. Larger building materials stores have a wide variety of cabinets from which to choose. Most are of standard size, but can be modified to fit specific requirements. Also select the mirror or medicine chest that will be installed above the cabinet. If you are refinishing your existing cabinets, select the stripper and finish you will use.

Step 3: Select the cabinet top and plumbing fixtures. Make sure that they fit your new or existing cabinet.

Step 4: Install the cabinet following the manufacturer's instructions. Most are pretty easy to install, leveling the unit and screwing the back of the cabinet into studs in the wall.

Step 5: Install the sink and faucet to the top. This is easier to do before you install the top on the cabinet.

Step 6: Install the cabinet top. Most are attached to the cabinet by metal clips from the inside of the cabinet. Others use screws that come up from the cabinet into the underside of the top. Make sure that the screws you use aren't too long as they could come up through the top's surface.

Step 7: Install the water lines and drain line and trap underneath the sink. Make sure all fittings are tight before turning the water back on.

Remodeling Bathroom Floors

Replacing bathroom floors is similar to installing new flooring in your kitchen (Chapter 6). Popular bathroom flooring materials include linoleum, vinyl, and ceramic tile. Wood flooring, which is susceptible to water damage, shouldn't be used unless it is completely sealed with a waterproof resin. Flooring comes in sheets (linoleum and vinyl) and squares (vinyl and ceramic).

The steps for remodeling your bathroom floor are essentially the same as those described in Chapter 6. Be sure, though, that you generously apply all adhesives and sealants. Bathroom flooring is more likely than kitchen flooring to be challenged by water spills and puddles. Here are the five steps for remodeling your bathroom floor.

Step 1: Prepare the old floor. Depending on what the new flooring material is, you must cover, remove, or at least roughen the old floor to accept adhesive. Remember that a new vinyl floor will emphasize any imperfections in the old floor, so consider first installing a new subfloor of $3/16$-inch plywood.

Step 2: Measure the floor to find the center of the room. Starting the flooring in the center of the room minimizes any differences of width between one end of the room and the other. Floors in smaller rooms can be started at one side if the walls are relatively parallel.

Step 3: Start laying the flooring. To start tile flooring, make a large cross at the center of the room and place the first four tiles at the *center* of the cross. To start sheet flooring, use the center of the room to align the design. You can also use large sheets of paper to first make a pattern of the floor, then transfer the pattern to the flooring sheets. The cut flooring sheet is then rolled up and moved to the new floor to be unrolled.

Step 4: Finish the edges. Whether flooring is in sheets or tiles, there will probably be some edging work to be done. You can cut sheet flooring with a flooring knife; floor tiles with a knife, saw, or hard tile cutter; wooden floor strips with a saw. You may first need to remove wood or plastic molding or edging.

Step 5: Clean up the work site. Remove all excess materials, adhesives, fasteners, and dirt. Then clean and finish the flooring. Scrub or mop the new floor surface as needed.

Remodeling Bathroom Walls

The walls in most bathrooms are covered by cabinets and fixtures, but remodeling them can still enhance the room. As you plan your bathroom remodeling job, consider how you can enhance it with changes to the walls.

☞ **Money-$aving Tip #26** *To minimize future mildew damage—and repair costs—consider adding or upgrading the vent fan or heating system. These changes will reduce mildew and increase comfort.*

Here are the five steps for remodeling your bathroom walls.

Step 1: Measure the height and width of the exposed wall surface in your bathroom.

Step 2: Select the most appropriate wall covering. Look for a covering that will be functional as well as offer the colors you want to use in your bathroom. Select a wall covering that will stand up well to the excess moisture in the bathroom. Options include plastic laminate, vinyl-coated wallpaper, semigloss enamel paint, plastic masonry blocks, or cast marble. The measurements from Step 1 will indicate how much material you will need.

Step 3: Prepare the wall surface. What this requires depends on the existing surface and the material for the new wall covering. Plastic laminate will need a clean, hard, dry surface for adhesion. Vinyl-coated wallpaper will need the underlying surface to be clean and dry. If necessary, install a thin (³⁄₁₆-inch) *exterior-grade* panel over the old surface for a clean and smooth surface that can stand up well in a moist environment.

Step 4: Install the wall covering. Make sure that any wallpaper seams will fall where they show the least. Also make sure that the pattern, if any, is level and aligned, especially for long stretches of wall where errors can be most obvious.

Step 5: Complete the job. Trim as needed. Install edging and molding. Clean the surface following the manufacturer's recommendations.

Remodeling Bathroom Doors and Windows

Many people who remodel the bathroom forget to include doors and windows in their new design. That's unfortunate because refinishing or replacing old doors and windows can dramatically enhance the room at relatively low cost. A new frosted window may add sunlight while retaining privacy. A new door can add fresh color and enhance the beauty of the room (see Figure 7.1).

FIGURE 7.1 Components of a Door Frame

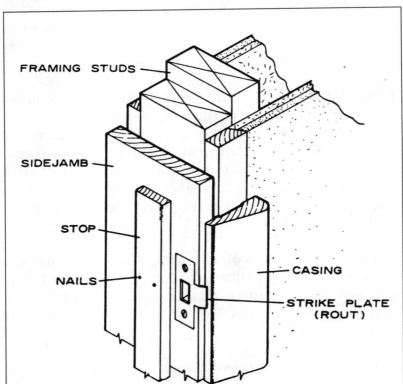

Here are the five steps for remodeling bathroom doors and windows.

Step 1: Inspect the door or window opening. Remove trim around the door and window to inspect the frame that holds the unit in place. Decide whether you need to replace the door only, door with hinges, or door and frame. In the case of a window, inspect the unit to decide how easy it will be to replace.

Step 2: Select the replacement unit. Your building materials retailer can help if you have all the dimensions and a drawing or picture of the door or window. Alternately, consider refinishing the existing unit. Aluminum window frames, for example, can be cleaned with an aluminum cleaner that will bring them back to life.

Step 3: Remove the old unit, then modify the opening as needed. In some cases, this means expanding or re-framing the opening to fit the new unit. Insulate around the opening to minimize heat loss.

Step 4: Install the new unit. Following manufacturer's instructions, place the new unit in the opening, shim as needed, and fasten it to the frame. Check to make sure you place it so that trim can easily be installed.

Step 5: Install the finish trim. If trim pieces need to be cut at an angle where they meet, use a miter box and saw to make the cut.

Other Bathroom Remodeling Ideas

Of course, there are dozens of other projects you can do or have your remodeling contractor do to enhance your bathroom. Here are a few of the most popular ones:

- As you are making changes, consider adding or upgrading the vent fan or heating system. If needed, add a wall or ceiling heater for additional comfort.
- Consider adding a light or skylight above the shower area for greater visibility and increased safety.
- If room allows, build a linen closet into the bathroom. Or build shelving above the toilet for linens.
- Consider adding a partition or wall to your bathroom to enhance privacy.

- If you have enough room, add a second sink to your cabinet to increase functionality.
- Be different. Curve wall corners that are now at 90-degree angles. Larger building materials retailers can show you how.
- Adding a second entry door to a bathroom can often enhance its functionality.

☞ **Money-$aving Tip #27** *To increase the storage space in your bathroom at a low cost, replace a hanging wall sink with a sink-and-cabinet unit of the same size.*

How Your Remodeler Can Help

Because bathroom remodeling is one of the most popular projects, many remodelers specialize in it. They have experience remodeling hundreds of bathrooms. Ask them for ideas. Sometimes remodelers can suggest a simple idea or two that greatly improves the room. Remodelers can also often suggest a decorating tip or two that, for a few extra dollars, makes the room more beautiful and relaxing. Whether you do it yourself or hire a professional, find a qualified remodeler who is willing to share ideas with you.

Commonly Asked Questions

Q. Should I replace older fixtures as I remodel?

A. Probably. The answer depends on whether the fixtures still work well and whether their design fit in with your bathroom's new look. In most cases, you should replace fixtures older than 10 years unless they are antiques.

Q. What can I do to make the bathroom look bigger?

A. Decorate to brighten the room. Add sunlight by removing curtains from windows, then fogging the glass with products from your building materials retailer or glass shop. Remove hardware, fixtures, and hanging plants you don't need. Sometimes simply replacing a large cabinet and mirror with a smaller unit to fit a smaller family can seemingly expand the bathroom.

Q. How can I keep mildew from forming in the bathroom?

A. Ventilate the bathroom with a fan and heater that allows wet surfaces to dry out. Also make sure that surfaces are nonporous to minimize the places where fungus can breed. Use a solution of bleachy water to wipe down surfaces where mildew can form, especially around showers and in bathroom window sills.

CHAPTER 8

Structural Remodeling

Sometimes you have to dig a little deeper.

It's true in life, and it's often true in remodeling your home. Remodeling may take more than replacing a fixture or cabinet. It may require that you change or repair the structure of your house.

This chapter can help. In the coming pages you'll learn how to inspect, analyze, estimate, and make common structural repairs and improvements to your home, including foundations, walls, ceilings, porches, and garages. You'll learn how professional remodelers work. Most important, this chapter will offer information to help you decide between doing it yourself or having it done.

Don't be intimidated by the thought of working on your home's structure. People do it all the time. So can you—once you know how.

Inspecting Your Home's Structure

Remodeling your home is the perfect event for looking at the structure of your home to make sure that it is in good condition for existing and future needs. As you have cabinets or fixtures out for replacement, you can inspect walls, floors, and other components to make sure they are sound.

An excellent book on this topic is the *CENTURY 21® Guide to Inspecting Your Home*. It thoroughly covers inspecting foundations, roofs, chimneys, fireplaces, exterior walls, windows, doors, mechanical systems, floors, and much more.

What to Look For

What will you be looking for as you inspect your home? Signs of wear and deterioration. Homes can be damaged by poor construction methods, age, insects, dampness, or nature.

Here are some of the things you will be looking for:

- Uneven floors
- Cracks in the home's foundation
- Piles of sawdust caused by wood-eating insects
- Doors and windows that don't close evenly, suggesting a frame out of alignment
- Doors that don't latch well
- Walls with bulges in them
- The smell of wet wood or insulation
- Loose roof shingles or tiles
- Exposed wood that is soft to the touch
- Masonry blocks, bricks, or mortar that crumbles easily
- Sagging or squeaking floors
- Heating units that don't work or aren't efficient
- Walls that tip in or out
- Cracks in plaster or drywall

- Standing water underneath the house
- Water stains on basement walls
- Decay in foundation or floor supports
- Nails popping up from drywall
- Porch flooring that is uneven
- Water stains on ceilings or interior walls
- Distorted cabinets or bulging soffits
- Damaged rain gutters or downspouts
- Evidence of leaking pipes or plumbing fixtures

Stepping Back

One of the best ways of looking for structural problems is to step back. You're in your home a lot. Plan to take a wider look at your home as you come home from work, shopping, or a vacation, when your eyes are fresher. Stand across the street or down the block and look at your home from all angles. Compare its lines to those of other homes in the neighborhood. Structural problems are typically large, such as a sagging roof line or one corner of the house lower than another. You may also see the cause of the problem, such as a damaged downspout that is letting water reach the foundation.

Take a look at your home from all angles. If you're friendly with neighbors, ask if you can inspect your home from their vantage point. You may see wall or roof damage that you cannot otherwise see. Do the same for them.

Getting Closer

Many large problems require closer inspection to find the cause. There are a couple of ways to do this. One is to use binoculars during your step-back inspection. Take a closer look at the roof line, downspout, foundation, and other structural components through binoculars.

The other option is to inspect your home from a few feet— or even a few inches—away. You may be closely checking out something you saw from across the street. Or you could be looking for structural problems that don't show up as easily from a distance. For example, use a garden trowel to remove dirt near the foundation, looking for insect nests and crumbling masonry.

You may also need to climb up into the attic to inspect the structure. You'll probably find an access door in the ceiling of one or more closets. Using a ladder, you can typically push the door up and to the side to access the area. From the ladder, you can use a flashlight to visually inspect the underside of the roof for water stains. You can also look for signs of insect damage.

When to Look

When is the best time to inspect the structure of your home? That depends. If you think there is damage from water and you're trying to find its source, the best time to inspect is when it's raining. Sorry. This is especially true if the source of the water isn't obvious.

For example, water damage to a bedroom may be from a roof leak. Accessing the area below the roof during a rainstorm can tell you lots. You may see that the source of the leak is a loose roof shingle. Water enters under the shingle, runs down a rafter and drips to a wall frame many feet away from the source.

Late spring and early fall are good times to inspect your home for the source of insect damage—if you can wait that long. You may see lots of activity around the foundation or roof of your home as the insects enter and exit.

Termites and other creatures love to live where people do: in the sunbelt. They dislike the coldest climates of the northern midwest United States, and so are most active in southern Texas, the south, and southern California. Though most modern homes in these areas are built to withstand such critters, not all are successful. So be especially sharp in inspecting homes there.

Estimating Structural Repairs

Structural problems can go deep. A soft spot in a concrete foundation can actually be caused by a crumbling footing underneath. Instead of a bag of cement, you may need part or all of the foundation replaced. That will probably require a second mortgage!

If you suspect structural problems, consider calling in an expert before you decide what repairs are needed. In fact, call in a couple of experts. A remodeling contractor or two may be able to give you good estimates. A contractor who specializes in such repairs can probably give you the most accurate estimate of the damage and costs to repair.

You can also estimate the job yourself. You can inspect the damage, do some research, and closely calculate the costs to repair. In fact, even if you think you'll probably hire a professional to actually do the repairs, you should make your own estimate of the job. Why? To be able to verify the contractor's bid and maybe even negotiate it.

How to Inspect Deeper

In most case, inspecting the structure of a home requires that someone get dirty. It could be you, a family member or friend, or the contractor. Whoever wins (or loses) the toss of the coin gets the job.

Tools for inspecting include a hammer and an old screwdriver. For example, crawl under the house and use the hammer to bang on floor joists to see if they crumble or are soft. A screwdriver can be pushed into soft wood to see how deep the problem goes. The hammer can also be used to test the firmness of a concrete or masonry foundation.

Common Causes and Cures

The causes of structural damage include poor construction, insects, and fungi. The cure for poor construction is replacement. For example, a foundation with a poor footing may need to be replaced with a new footing and foundation section. A roof without adequate framing will need to be rebuilt, preferably by a contractor who can calculate load and stress to design a better roof system.

Termites and Ants

As mentioned earlier, termites and ants can cause many problems to structures that aren't built to withstand them. Modern building codes are written to minimize damage from these critters. Unfortunately, these codes aren't always enforced. Nor are older homes brought "up to code." And maybe a previous owner of your home hasn't followed the code when remodeling.

Subterranean termites are the enemy (see Figure 8.1). They live in the ground, crawling up into and eating the home's wood. So building the home with barriers that stop the termites from crawling up to the wood will minimize damage.

There are many ants, such as so-called carpenter ants, that eat wood in homes. They build nests in exposed and untreated wood, then eat their surroundings. Though homes can be built to withstand such insects, periodic treatment to destroy their nests is also needed in some regions of the country.

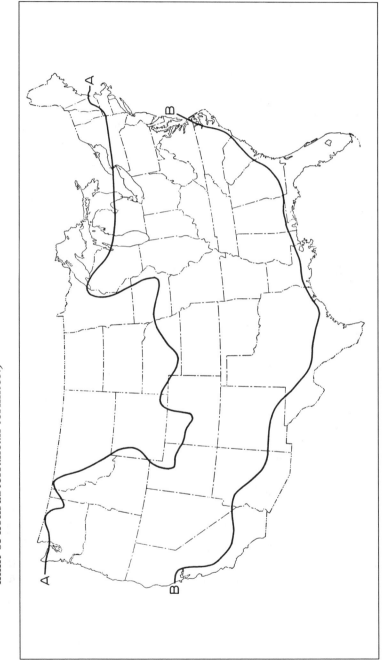

FIGURE 8.1 Where Termites Live. ("A" is the northern limit of subterranean termites. "B" is the northern limit of nonsubterranean termites.)

Mildew and Fungi

Wood decay is caused by fungi that live in and eat wood. Advanced decay is easily recognized. It is brown and crumbly or white and spongy. Unfortunately, by the time the wood shows decay, it is probably beyond repair and needs replacement.

The key to minimizing structural damage from mildew and fungi is to keep wood dry. If wood becomes wet, it must be able to drain the water away easily so that standing water doesn't feed the problem. What's commonly called "dry rot" should really be called "wet rot" because it requires moisture to rot.

Making Structural Repairs

As a homeowner with a hammer and an optimistic attitude, you can make many of your own structural repairs. This chapter covers many such repairs, offering step-by-step instruction for doing so. Remember, however, that these instructions are guidelines that apply to repairing the typical home. Your home may vary, so really do your homework before trying any of this at home!

Tools You'll Need

Tools needed for making structural repairs vary, of course. If you're simply replacing a few concrete blocks, some mortar tools will probably be enough. If you're replacing the roof and gutters, a hammer will be your main tool. For some other tasks you'll want a power saw or other power tools. We'll cover them under the specific repairs.

Materials You'll Need

Replacement materials for structural remodeling are easy to identify. That is, you replace damaged 2 × 8 framing with a new 2 × 8, and damaged ⅜-inch drywall with new ⅜-inch drywall. Besides the replacement materials, you'll need fasteners such as nails, screws, and adhesives. Your building materials supplier can recommend the type and amount you'll need.

Skills You'll Need

What skills will you need to make structural repairs to your home? Chapter 4 covered them. Most structural repairs require that you have skills in carpentry and masonry, depending on the job.

Do you have these skills? If not, either practice or hire. You can also choose to hire help for those skills you'd prefer not (or don't have time) to learn. For example, you may replace damaged drywall but prefer to hire someone to clean or install gutters.

It's your home. You call the shots.

Repairing the Foundation

The name tells you a home's foundation is a vital part of its structure. Without a good foundation, houses crumble and fall. Fortunately, most repair work on a home's foundation is minor.

Minor hairline cracks are found in the foundation of most homes. They typically don't require repair. A problem occurs when small cracks allow water to seep in and make them big cracks or let moisture into other parts of the home. Problems can also occur if there isn't enough slope around the foundation to allow for drainage (see Figure 8.2).

FIGURE 8.2 Make Sure Water Drains Away from Foundation
Walls

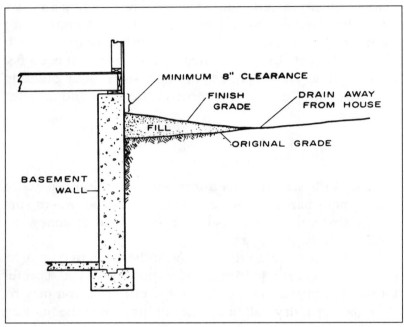

Here are the three steps for repairing a foundation.

Step 1: Inspect the damage. If it doesn't require imme-
diate repair, mark the crack with a pencil or colored pen
and look at it again in a few weeks.

Step 2: If necessary, repair the crack. Cracks that are
stable can be patched with a foundation or concrete patch
available from building materials stores. Active cracks require an elastic sealant from the same source. Clean away any
loose mortar before making the repair.

***Step 3: If the foundation needs further repair,
consider calling a contractor.*** In some cases, the house
must be jacked up, portions of the footing and foundation

removed and replaced. This is typically not a job for the do-it-yourselfer.

Repairing Walls

Walls are vital to your home's integrity. Structurally, there are two types of walls: load-bearing and non-load-bearing. As you might have guessed, load-bearing walls are required to support the weight of whatever is above it. Non-load-bearing walls don't.

How can you tell which walls in your home are load-bearing? You'll be right most of the time if you simply imagine your home's structure if a specific wall were removed. If the wall between the two rooms was removed, for example, would the house fall down? In single-story homes, there is usually at least one wall through the center of the home that runs parallel to the front of the house. This one is usually load-bearing. It goes and the house goes. Other walls perpendicular (right angle) to it will usually be non-load-bearing walls.

The point here is not to make you a structural engineer, but to help you look at each wall in your home as more than just a room divider. Some walls also hold up the roof, while others aren't required to do so. That means repairing a load-bearing wall is more serious than repairing one that doesn't carry a heavy load.

Fortunately, many of the repairs needed to walls don't require their removal.

Here are the three steps for repairing walls.

Step 1: Inspect the wall for damage. If there is simply a hole in the wall, you can probably repair it without much effort. If there are large cracks in the wall or the top is buckling, the damage is deeper.

Step 2: To repair a hole in a drywall wall, purchase a patch kit at a building materials retailer. The kit will include a thin mesh that covers the hole and some plaster that is smoothly spread over the mesh. Once dry, sand the plaster carefully so it is smooth with the surrounding wall, then paint as needed.

Step 3: If the wall has structural damage, consider calling in a contractor. The problem may be caused by poor construction. If you plan to make the repair yourself, refer to *The New Complete Home Repair Manual* by the Editors of Consumer Guide (847-676-3470) or similar comprehensive books on home repairs.

Repairing Ceilings

The two most common repairs made to ceilings are replacing an area that is stained by water and one that is sagging. In both cases, the damage is typically caused by water leaking from either the roof or upstairs plumbing. In either case, the repair begins with repairing the *cause* of the problem.

Here are the three steps for repairing ceilings (see Figure 8.3).

Step 1: Inspect the ceiling for damage. If necessary, remove some of the ceiling to determine the cause of the damage (e.g., leaky bathtub plumbing leaking onto the living room ceiling). Repair the source of the water leak as needed.

Step 2: To repair a hole in a drywall ceiling, purchase a ceiling patch kit at a building materials retailer. The kit includes a mesh to cover the hole and plaster to cover the mesh. Repaint or retexture the ceiling as needed.

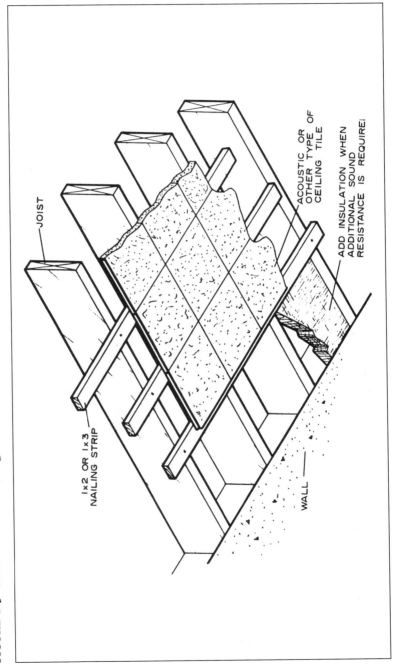

FIGURE 8.3 Installation of Ceilings

☞ **Money-$aving Tip #28** *If you're repairing a hole in a drywall ceiling yourself, make sure you buy a repair kit made specifically for ceilings rather than walls. The mesh for ceiling repairs is stiffer to hold the weight of the plaster.*

Step 3: To repair a suspended ceiling, push the damaged panel up then to one side, tip and remove it from the frame. Take the unit to a building materials retailer for an exact replacement. If the other panels are aged, consider replacing all panels at the same time to minimize color differences.

Repairing Roofs and Gutters

Repairing or replacing a roof is not a difficult job—unless heights bother you. In that case, a safety rope and the buddy system can minimize, but not eliminate your fear of falling. It may be wiser to have a professional roofer do the job for you.

☞ **Money-$aving Tip #29** *Before you decide to repair or replace a roof, determine the extent of the job—partial or full. Also, if you're going to use a professional remodeler, you may be able to save money by combining roof repair and other home remodeling jobs.*

Gutters are another matter. Gutters can be replaced on single-story homes using a 6-foot step ladder.

Here are the four steps for repairing a roof (see Figure 8.4).

Step 1: Inspect the roof. In some cases, the problem may simply be a loose shingle that allows water to seep in. In other cases, a section of plywood and roofing must be replaced.

FIGURE 8.4 Installation of Roofing

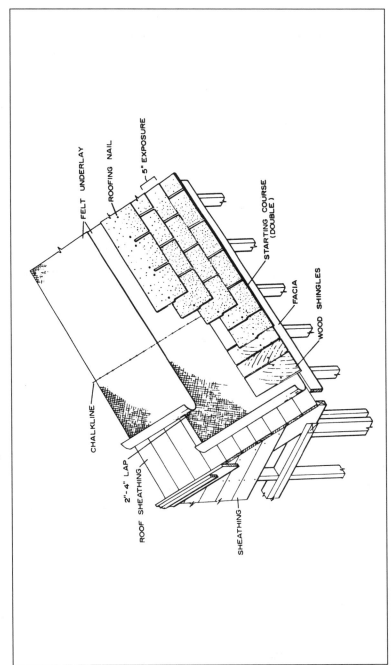

Step 2: To install a new roof or section of a roof, remove shingles as necessary. You can remove asphalt shingles by pushing pitch fork tines under the bottom edge to lift the shingle and nails.

Step 3: Replace old roofing paper with new paper. Overlap as needed.

Step 4: Replace roof shingles or tiles. Use standard roofing nails or a staple gun designed for the job.

Here are the three steps for repairing gutters (see Figure 8.5).

Step 1: Inspect the gutters. Some gutters need only patching with a fiberglass or metal patch kit. Others simply need accumulated vegetation cleaned out.

Step 2: To replace a gutter, pull the long nails that attach the outer edge of the gutter to the roof board or fascia. Purchase or cut replacement gutters the same length as the old ones. Install using new gutter nails.

Step 3: To replace downspouts, remove the elbow from below the gutter. The elbow is held in place by friction or a set screw. Check to see if cleaning debris from the pipes will solve the problem. If not, replace the downspout and elbow with exact replacement parts available at building materials stores. You may need to replace straps holding the gutter against the house.

Repairing Porches

Porches are regaining interest in new home construction. In addition, many older homes are being remodeled with repaired or replaced porches. You may be able to repair your own home's porch.

FIGURE 8.5 Installation of Gutter and Downspout

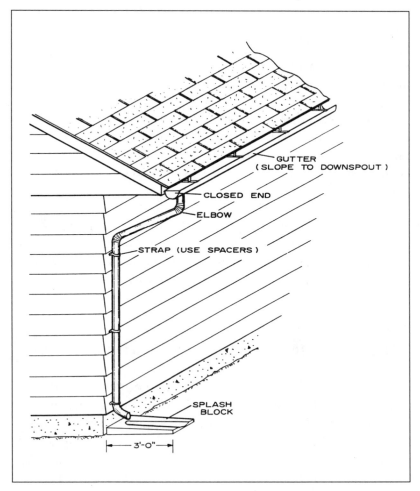

Here are the three steps for repairing a porch.

Step 1: Identify the problem. In some cases, a sagging porch is caused by a foundation block that has moved off its footing. In others, a post has rotted away and needs replacement. In still other situations, the entire porch must be replaced.

Step 2: To replace a foundation block on its footing, use a small house jack to raise the porch frame near the footing. It must be raised high enough to replace the block on the footing. If the block is sound, reinstall it squarely and evenly on the footing. If you have any doubt about the block's soundness, replace it.

Step 3: To replace a sagging porch, remove materials (boards, posts, rails). Pour new cement footings and install new foundation blocks. Install new wooden joists of at least the same dimensions as the old ones. Then install replacement materials.

☞ **Money-$aving Tip #30** *If you're replacing a sagging porch on an older home, remove and reuse what you can of the existing materials. It can both save you money and make your home look like a classic home.*

How Your Remodeler Can Help

If you're trying to save money on your remodeling job by doing some of the repairs yourself, discuss it with your remodeling contractor. There are some jobs you can easily do yourself, while others require special tools and skills. In addition, you may find that some of the planned repairs are unnecessary because the remodeling will redo the repaired area anyway.

Commonly Asked Questions

Q. What should I do about a sagging roofline?

A. Cry. In most cases, a sagging roofline means that there are structural problems with the house. The foundation may be crumbling. An interior load-bearing wall may need repairs. The roof system may need rebuilding. None of these jobs are cheap. Have a professional home inspector help you figure out the cause of the sag and suggest a solution.

Q. Should I repair or replace old plaster on walls?

A. That depends. If you're only repairing a small portion of a plastered wall, the best bet is probably to replaster that part of the wall. However, if you must resurface an entire plaster wall, consider covering it with drywall if it is more decorative or less expensive to do so.

Q. Should I consider vinyl siding?

A. Vinyl siding is a long-lasting solution for many homes, minimizing maintenance and adding to the value of a home. However, vinyl siding is not cheap. If you plan to stay in your home at least long enough for its value to appreciate to recoup the cost of the siding, consider doing so. Your best option is to set aside money to pay for it rather than pay for the siding on credit.

CHAPTER 9

Adding and Changing Rooms

Sometimes, remodeling a room isn't enough. Your home may need substantially more space—or at least a revision of functions: a garage becomes a bedroom, a utility room becomes a second bathroom.

You're talking major remodeling here.

You can do it yourself or you can pay a remodeler. But to make the best choice, you first need to know what's involved in adding or changing a room in your home. That's what this chapter is about.

In the coming pages you'll learn how to design, add, and modify rooms in your home for more usability. This chapter includes specific information on adding a bedroom and bath, remodeling or expanding an existing room, and converting a garage into living space.

Get your planning paper out and let's make some changes.

Considering Adding a Room

When space runs out in your home—elderly relatives move in with you, the stork drops a bundle down the chimney—adding a room on to your home is a strong option. A 120-square-foot bedroom, for example, can really increase living space. Or a new 60-square-foot bathroom can relieve morning stress. Adding a room may seem to be the best option.

What's involved in adding a room to your home? Much depends on the current design of your home. Adding a room may mean building a room at an existing exterior doorway. It can also mean increasing the floor space on a second story by lifting the roof line and installing a dormer.

In most cases, adding a room requires some structural changes to your house. You may need to punch a doorway into an interior or exterior wall. Or you may pour a foundation where your roses were. Consider very carefully adding a room.

☞ **Money-$aving Tip #31** *Talk first with an architect or at least a contractor who can look at your home's design with educated eyes. These professionals can often see options that you could never have considered. They can also tell you about potential problems that could add thousands of dollars to the costs of adding a room.*

Take your time. Get good advice. Consider the costs and the benefits. Make wise decisions.

Considering Changing a Room

You usually have more than one option. Instead of adding a new room to your home, you can change the function of one or more rooms. For example, you can convert an unfinished attic area into a bedroom. Or it can become a more efficient storage area, freeing up room on the main floor for living space. A formal dining area can become part of the kitchen. Or, if you don't do much formal entertaining, you can convert the dining room to a study. In some areas, attic bedrooms may have special requirements or even be illegal. Check your local building codes before starting such a project.

Many people consider converting all or part of a garage into extra living space. It's easier to ask a car to sleep outside than to ask one of the family members or guests to do so. It's an easy option, but it isn't always the best one. Why? Because some homebuyers consider converted garages a negative feature or will not consider purchasing a home without a garage.

☞ **Money-$aving Tip #32** *Before planning to convert a garage into living space, consider whether you will soon be selling your home and how it will impact the value. Ask for your real estate agent's professional opinion on garage remodeling.*

That doesn't mean you can't remodel a portion of the garage to gain added living space. If nothing else, most garages can be modified to increase their amount of storage space, which can, in turn, free up space in the home. Think about it.

Designing New Rooms

So how does one (specifically *you*) go about designing a new room in your home? Again, consider hiring professional help with this task. Unless you know quite a bit about architecture and construction, you could make design errors that will wipe out any savings on design fees.

Here are the five steps for designing a new room.

Step 1: Calculate your needs. Decide the function of the new room (sleeping, bathing, office, etc.) and figure out how much space you will need. You can do this by determining the intended room's needs in terms of number of people who will use it and the furnishings they'll require. Then compare this information with the size of other rooms and how they accommodate people and furnishings.

Step 2: Decide where to add the room. Does the room's function require that it be in one part of the home more so than another? Should it be with other bedrooms or share a plumbing wall with another bath? Must it have outside access for business clients?

Step 3: Plan the room. With the help of an architect or remodeling contractor, draw plans for the room including how it will be added to the existing structure. Consider all systems: electrical, structural, plumbing, heating and cooling, etc.

Step 4: Plan the project. Make your decision to either do it yourself of hire the remodeling out to a contractor. If outside funding is needed, develop full plans that can be presented to the lender.

Step 5: Start the project. If you're hiring a remodeling contractor, work out all the terms and get it in writing. If you're doing it yourself, select your primary materials supplier, establish an account, get needed permits, and start construction.

Modifying Existing Rooms

As discussed earlier in this chapter, sometimes the best option is to modify an existing room to new purposes. A utility room often becomes a second or third bathroom. A garage is partially or fully converted into living space. You have many opportunities, many options.

Here are the five steps for modifying an existing room.

Step 1: Calculate your needs. Determine the new function of the existing room and calculate how much space is available. You may decide to remodel an existing room to serve more than one function, such as changing a double-car garage into a bedroom with bath and a single-car garage.

Step 2: Decide which existing room you will change. Depending on the new room's function, it may need to be in one part of your home over another. Or it may need to be close to a stairway or a bathroom. Choose the best location for your modified room.

Step 3: Plan the room. Get help from an architect or remodeling contractor in drawing the existing room then drawing how the room will be changed to fit the new purposes. Remember to consider all systems: electrical, structural, plumbing, heating and cooling, etc.

Step 4: Plan the project. Make your decision to either do it yourself of hire the remodeling out to a contractor. If you need a loan to fund the remodeling project, you'll need full plans and an estimate of the value of your home after the remodeling is completed.

Step 5: Start the project. If you're using a remodeling contractor, get all terms in writing. If you're doing it yourself, select your materials suppliers, establish an account, get necessary building permits, and start construction.

Adding a Bedroom

One of the most popular additions is a bedroom. Families expand. Siblings who used to get along well hit a certain age and can't stand to be within 11 feet of each other. Grandparents move in. It's time to add a bedroom.

Here are the seven steps for adding a bedroom.

Step 1: Plan the room. Calculate the space needed, including closets. Decide where the room needs lighting, switches, electrical and phone outlets, and other services.

Step 2: As required, install the footing and foundation for the new bedroom. Make sure the foundation conforms to local building codes and that you have proper permits.

Step 3: Install floor joists and subflooring per plans. Then install wall and roof framing. Make sure the new room fits in with the design of the existing structure.

Step 4: Install exterior siding and roofing to protect the room from the elements. You may need to reside or reroof some of the existing structure so that the new room merges smoothly with the home.

Step 5: Install electrical wiring and heating as needed. This will require a licensed electrician and maybe a heating contractor.

Step 6: Finish the interior walls and ceiling with insulation and drywall (see Figure 9.1). Finish the floor with hardwood, tile, or carpet, as planned.

Step 7: Finish and decorate to taste.

FIGURE 9.1 How to Tape Drywall Joints

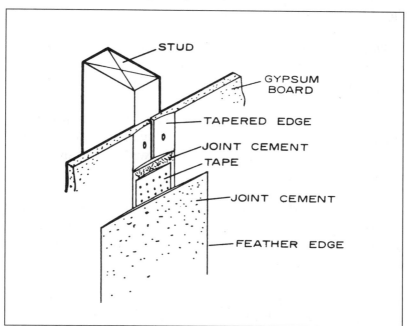

Adding a Bathroom

Adding a bathroom to your home is similar to adding a bedroom, except that plumbing the room for fixtures is a major part of the job. Adding a bathroom to your home can offer both convenience and value.

☞ **Money-$aving Tip #33** *Consider adding a small hot water heater to your new bathroom, especially if the room is located very far from the existing hot water heater.*

Whether you do it yourself or hire a remodeler, here are the eight steps for adding a bathroom.

Step 1: Plan the room. Calculate the space needed for specific fixtures (tub, shower, toilet, cabinet, storage, etc.).

Decide where the room needs fresh water pipes, drain lines, lighting, switches, electrical outlets, and other services.

Step 2: As required, install the footing and foundation for the new bathroom. Check building codes and get permits for the new foundation, room, and services.

Step 3: Install floor joists and subflooring following the bathroom's plans. Then install wall and roof framing, making sure the new bathroom fits in with the design of the existing structure.

Step 4: Install exterior siding and roofing to protect the room from the elements. This may require re-siding or reroofing some of the existing structure so that the new bathroom merges smoothly with the home.

Step 5: Install plumbing. Do it yourself or use a licensed plumber or remodeling contractor.

Step 6: Install electrical wiring and heating as needed. You will probably need a licensed electrician and a heating contractor.

Step 7: Finish the interior walls and ceiling with insulation and drywall. Finish the floor as planned.

Step 8: Install cabinets, sinks, toilet, tub, shower, and other fixtures as needed.

Converting a Garage

Converting all or part of an attached garage into living space offers the benefit of not having to install a foundation, walls, and roof. Those components are already in place. The disadvantage is that you lose some or all of your garage. You can overcome this disadvantage by building a separate garage (if space allows), or remodeling your home for storing some of the things normally stored in your garage. A shed in the backyard can be the new home of your lawn and garden equipment and shop tools. Or you may decide to make part of your existing garage more efficient.

Here are the five steps for converting a garage.

Step 1: Plan the conversion. Take measurements of your existing garage, then figure out how you will use the space most efficiently. A single-car garage may become a family room or bedroom and an extra bathroom. A double-car garage can become a single-car garage with an extra room or two. Make sure you get the needed permits and follow local building codes.

Step 2: Remove wall framing and other components. Then install new doorways and windows following your plans (see Figure 9.2).

Step 3: Add electrical and plumbing services as needed. An electrician should be involved in the planning and installation to make sure it conforms to local building codes. Don't forget to plan and install an adequate heating system and insulation.

Step 4: Add interior walls as needed (see Figure 9.3). Finish all walls with drywall. Finish floors with subflooring and tile, carpet, hardwood, or other flooring.

Step 5: Finish the project. Add fixtures, interior doors, and other components and decorate to taste.

FIGURE 9.2 How to Frame a Window

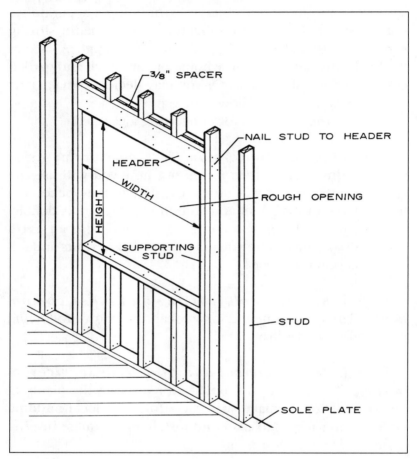

Converting an Attic

In many homes, the attic is wasted space that can be re-modeled into quality living space. In other homes, the attic can be finished off to serve as storage to free up space in the home for living.

FIGURE 9.3 How to Install an Interior Wall

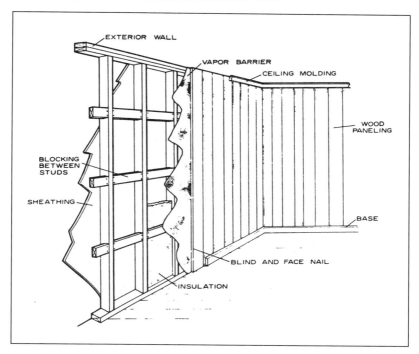

Here are the five steps for converting an attic.

Step 1: Plan the conversion. Take measurements of your existing attic, then figure out how you will use the space most efficiently. A short attic with no space to stand up will require that the roof be raised to at least 7 feet above the attic floor. Some attics may also require the installation of flooring materials. Make sure your plans follow local building codes and get required permits before construction begins.

Step 2: As needed, install flooring so you can work in the attic area. Then make changes to the roof, adding a dormer and walls to increase living space. You may also need to install new windows and doorways following your plans. Make sure you have good access to the attic through a stairway.

Step 3: Add electrical and plumbing services as needed. An electrician should be involved in the planning and installation to make sure everything conforms to local building codes. Don't forget to plan and install an adequate heating system and insulation to the attic room, especially between the ceiling and the roof where heat can be trapped.

Step 4: Add interior walls as needed. Finish all walls with drywall. Finish floors with subflooring and tile, carpet, hardwood, or other flooring.

Step 5: Finish the project. Add fixtures, interior doors, and other components and decorate to taste.

How Your Remodeler Can Help

A qualified remodeling contractor can help you find an architect who is experienced in designing new rooms and conversions. If an architect isn't necessary, the contractor may be able to help you draw up plans that will save you time and money in your addition or conversion.

Commonly Asked Questions

Q. Does converting a garage to an extra room increase or decrease home value?

A. It depends on how well the job is done and what is lost in the process. A quality conversion can increase the livability and the value of a home, especially if a new garage is built to replace the space lost from the converted garage.

Q. What can I do to reduce the heat in an attic so it is livable?

A. Insulate like crazy. There are quality insulators with high R-factors that can be installed between an attic roof and ceiling. Cross-ventilation using fans can be effective. Also consider redirecting air-conditioning from below through the attic for additional cooling.

Q. How can I add attic access?

A. If the attic will only be used for storage, a simple pull-down stairway can be purchased from a building materials retailer and installed in an existing attic access hole. Otherwise, consider installing or extending a stairway, making sure that the slope of the stairs isn't too steep.

CHAPTER 10

Remodeling Your Yard

Yes, you can remodel your yard!

In fact, your yard may be the best place to start your remodeling venture. It's easy. It's rewarding. It's fun.

In this chapter, you'll learn how to remodel your home by adding or improving outdoor living space at low cost. The coming pages include specific information on selecting and installing landscaping, fences, decks, and outdoor storage structures that add value to your home.

Considering Your Yard

There are four things you should consider as you remodel your home's landscaping: nature, harmony, concealment, and maintenance. Let's look at each of them.

First, consider nature. Here are some questions to ask:

- Will the fence, trees, or shrubs change the amount of sunlight received within your yard?
- Will they increase shade?
- Will they redirect or stop the wind?
- How much and during what part of the year?
- Are these changes advantages or disadvantages to your yard's intended use?
- Will a planned tree drop leaves into the pool?
- Will a tall, windbreaking fence cast too much shade into your garden area?
- Will the shrubs next to the fence receive adequate light and water?

Second, make sure there is harmony of purpose and of design:

- Will the ground cover blend in with your stone wall or will it detract?
- Are the colors of the flowers complementary to your home?

Concealment refers to landscape elements that cover something else: a fence, a rock, or a view. You might choose ivy to conceal a fence. A tree that grows quite full could be planted to conceal a view. Make sure that the concealment serves its purpose. It's a waste of time and money to install a quality fence or shed and then plant climbers that completely cover it. Instead, use climbers to conceal an unattractive fence.

Whether the landscape element is a fence, hedge, or ground cover, it should not require undue maintenance. Some ivies can take over a yard in a couple seasons and be a chore to maintain. Other plants can thrive on neglect.

Selecting Trees

Trees act as natural barriers that add beauty and function to a yard. Trees can offer both effective noise control and shade.

Shade trees should ideally be a sturdy, long-lived species, one that in a relatively short time produces the size and shape desired. Keep in mind the probable *mature* height and spread of any trees you select. If yours is a one-story house on a small lot, you should plant small trees.

Consider the planting site and its soil type, compaction, and drainage. Climate is critical too. Many species when planted north of their adapted range are killed by early fall or late spring frosts.

☞ **Money-Saving Tip #34** *To ensure that you don't have to replace new trees in a year, select only those trees that will be hardy enough to survive summer heat and winter cold in your area. Your local garden shop or land-scaper can give you information about your region.*

In newly established yards, it's a good idea to fertilize your plants every year until they are established. Liquid pre-mix fertilizers are available at garden centers. These fertilizers are advantageous in that they are available immediately to the plant, and no fertilizer residue is left to burn the plants roots or grass. Follow the directions on the label when applying these fertilizers.

Selecting Shrubs

Shrubs can be planted in the same way as trees to define your property, reduce noise, and increase beauty in your yard. Evergreen plants generally keep their leaves year-round and often make the best hedges. Semi-evergreens might lose some of their foliage during the fall and winter.

Deciduous plants drop their leaves during colder months and are used where winter shade is not needed.

☞ **Money-$aving Tip #35** *To ensure healthier land-scaping, plant evergreen shrubs in the fall or spring and deciduous shrubs in the spring.*

Selecting Flowers

You can remodel your yard with the beauty and color of flowers. You can tie together the color of the house and out-door living area, or you can separate them with the appro-priate selection of perennials, annuals, and bulbs.

Perennials are long-lived, strong growers that produce richly colored flowers. Popular perennials include aster, baby's breath, carnation, chrysanthemum, columbine, del-phinium, hibiscus, iris, lily of the valley, peony, primrose, sunflower, and violet.

Annuals can bring colorful blooms to your yard on little notice, especially during seasons when perennials are dor-mant. Common annuals include African daisy, baby blue-eyes, California poppy, everlasting, forget-me-not, French marigold, nasturtium, petunia, snapdragon, sweet pea, and tassel flower.

Bulbs are the trumpets of spring, offering bright colors and varied designs. Common bulbs are crocus, dahlia, glory-of-the-snow, hyacinth, lily of the nile, narcissus, star-of-Beth-lehem, tulip, and wind-flower.

Selecting Ground Covers

Ground covers serve as natural carpeting for outdoor activities and help fill in landscaping with easy-maintenance beauty. Ground covers include bog-rosemary, carmel creeper, cinquefoil, creeping mahonia, dwarf rosemary, English ivy, ground holly, ground ivy, Hall's honeysuckle, ice plant, pachysandra, periwinkle, rock spray, Scotch heather, star jasmine, sweet fern, thyme, wild strawberry, and wintercreeper.

The most popular ground cover is lawn grasses. They are classified into two groups: cold-season (for areas with winter frost and snow) and subtropical (for areas with milder winters). Cold-season grasses include bents, bluegrasses, clover, coarse fescues, fine fescues, red top, and rye grasses. Subtropical grasses include Bermuda grasses, Saint Augustine grass, and zoysia grasses.

Selecting Landscaping Rocks

You can creatively use rocks as landscaping elements in many ways. They can be grouped to form rock gardens. You can bury flat rocks to become the tops of walkway steps. Rocks can be the central point of a landscape design.

A true rock garden is not a haphazard collection of rocks sprinkled with plants, but it has distinctive characteristics. The rocks should be native to your locality and blended with natural plants.

Selecting Yard Lighting

One of the most dramatic decorations you can add to your yard is lighting. You can use your fence as the backdrop or screen for many shadows and designs by running underground wires and setting spotlights. You can accent the wood or masonry texture, silhouette plants or decorations, spotlight a fountain, or even add color lighting for special effects.

Electric wiring for outside lighting must be weatherproof and must follow the National Electrical Code and code of local regulatory agencies.

☞ **Money-$aving Tip #36** *Weatherproof electrical components are a little more expensive than interior electrical materials, but they are less expensive than replacing weather-damaged components every year or two.*

New installations use a floodlight holder for incandescent lamps (bulbs) with built-in reflectors. Some types completely shield the lamp, permitting the use of indoor lamps. Others shield only the lamp base, and outdoor or weatherproof lamps must be used. Although not as efficient as other types of higher-wattage lamps, incandescent lamps are used where the lamps are turned off and on frequently. Make sure you install a lighting switch or timer where it can be easily accessed.

Tungsten-halogen incandescent lamps have a longer life and are used in larger-wattage floodlights. Tungsten-halogen is normally a tubular lamp with electric contacts at each end, although some are available in reflector types with regular screw bases.

You can use fluorescent lamps for outdoor lighting provided that you use a weatherproof fixture, that the lamps are enclosed with a transparent cover for temperatures below 50°F, and that you use special ballasts or fixtures for operation at below-freezing temperatures. A fluorescent lamp's light output efficiency at indoor temperatures is normally two to three times that of an incandescent. The efficiency is only slightly more than incandescent lamps for outdoor temperatures of freezing or below.

Torches that burn kerosene or similar fuels are decorative and portable for occasional outdoor use in patios and gardens. Be sure to keep open torches away from combustible materials.

Hiring a Landscape Contractor

You might decide to have some or all of the landscaping done for you by professionals. You could design it yourself and have a landscape contractor do the work, or have it drawn up by a landscape architect or designer and let him or her subcontract the job to a landscaper.

The cost of full landscaping is usually figured at about 5 percent of the home's value. A $150,000 home will probably need about $7,500 in landscaping to bring up the quality of the home. This figure might be on the high side depending on the size of the lot, whether the construction of a fence or masonry walls is included, and what outdoor structures are planned.

Do your homework on any landscaping firm you're considering hiring. Ask for local client references and visit or call them to assess the quality of the firm's work. Also ask the landscaper for business references (bank, subcontractors, suppliers) and only work with an all-around reputable firm. Make sure the contractor is bonded and has adequate liability insurance in case your property is damaged or any worker is hurt on the job while on your property.

Also consider using a landscape retailer or nursery that will design your landscaping at no charge if you buy your plants and materials from them.

Here's another tip: know what you're getting. A reputable landscape contractor, designer, or architect will provide you with detailed plot drawings, artist renditions, and a list of plants, shrubs, and trees that will be installed. Make sure the written contract includes when work will begin, when it will be completed, what happens if it isn't completed on time (forfeiture of partial funds), how it will be paid for, and who has final say-so. Of course, local weather conditions may change the project's timetable without prior approval. Depending on the complexity of the job and total price, you might want a lawyer to look over the contract.

Installing Fences

One of the most popular outdoor remodeling projects is installing a fence. Fences are simply walls intended to impede wind, snow, light, vision, or animals on their appointed rounds. Fences are easily built of basic building materials—wood, fasteners, and finish. Yet each fence has its own purpose and personality. Some are decorative and quaint, while others are massive and impenetrable.

The first thing to do after you have decided to build a fence is to check your local zoning regulations. Most areas have rules about fence heights, property line setbacks, and aesthetics. Check your property deed as well because some include restrictions and reservations that may affect your fence plan.

Next, review your boundary survey. If you don't have an up-to-date survey of your property's boundaries, consider having it done before you begin installing a permanent structure. A few dollars spent on a survey can save much embarrassment and possible legal problems. To allow for survey errors, plan to install the fence several inches inside the boundary. Discuss your plans with connecting property owners. They may be interested in sharing the cost of installing and maintaining a fence directly on the property line because it adds to the value of their home as well. When you've reached agreement, remember to confirm everything *in writing* so there are no misunderstandings.

Good fence planning also includes checking for the location of utility lines and water pipes. Your survey should show the locations of utility easements, paths that underground utilities can use to reach your home and others within the neighborhood. Check your phone book under "Utilities"—as many local utility boards have united to offer free information about utility lines.

One of the initial purposes of fencing was security. We no longer must secure property from wild animals and invading hordes, but there still are real threats from burglars, vicious pets, and bill collectors. These considerations must be realized before the first post hole is dug.

Of more modern interest is the privacy fence (see Figure 10.1). With enlarging suburbs and shrinking lots, privacy is becoming more difficult to find and maintain. Fencing can help. Carefully planned and placed fencing can dramatically reduce vision to and from neighbors' yards, streets, and sidewalks. Good privacy fence planning includes making sure the fence architecture adds to rather than detracts from the home's architecture.

Selecting Fence Materials

The selection of materials is as important as the design. Good materials can double the life of your fence and reduce the lifetime cost dramatically. After choosing the style and height of the fence you want to build, the next step is to estimate how much lumber or other materials you will need.

To estimate materials, first draw a simple sketch of your backyard on a piece of graph paper (available at stationery stores). Draw the location of your planned fence or fences. Then use another sheet of graph paper to draw a typical section of your fence using a scale of ½ inch equals 1 foot. Calculate the materials needed to build one fence section and multiply it by the number of sections you will construct. List wood and hardware components separately. Make sure hardware and metal fencing are galvanized to minimize rust.

Setting Posts

Once you've designed your fence and selected materials, construction begins with setting posts. Typically, posts are one-third longer than the above-ground height. That is, a 6-foot high fence should be constructed of 8-foot long posts. Of course, much depends on the weight of the fence, the size of the posts, and local frost conditions.

FIGURE 10.1 Common Board Fence Designs

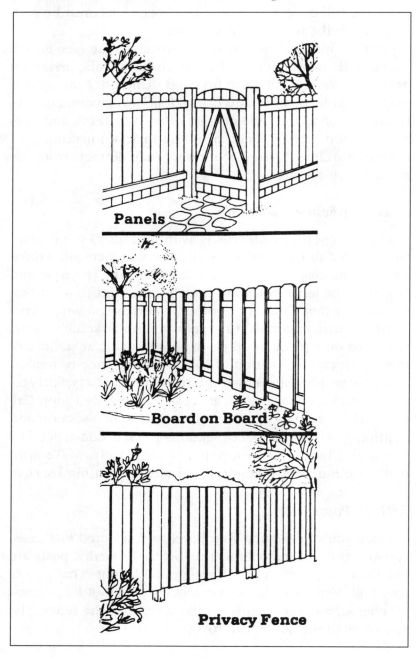

FIGURE 10.2 Installing a Fence Post in Concrete

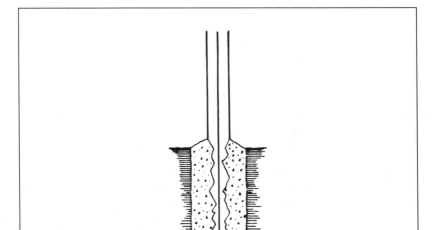

Fill the bottom of the post hole with gravel to a height of 6 inches. Gravel will allow water to drain away from the post, minimizing rotting and freezing damage. Fill the hole with concrete. Crown the concrete to encourage water to run away from the post (see Figure 10.2).

Installing Rail Fences

The simplest form of fencing is the rail fence. It is made with 6- to 12-foot horizontal rails spanned between posts, normally 48 inches or shorter. Rail fences are popular for keeping in livestock and marking boundaries. They were extremely popular with early American settlers who simply split logs and set them between short posts.

The split-rail fence is made of so-called line posts installed approximately 8 to 10 inches apart at 10-foot intervals.

Twelve-foot rails are then placed between the posts so that the end of one rests on the end of another from the next fence section. Finally, a wire is wound between the line posts for stability and to discourage the removal of rails.

The post-and-board fence is more modern in design and is seen in many suburban areas, especially in front yards of homes in the western United States. It marks lot boundaries and minimizes lawn traffic without obstructing view or hampering grass cutting. The posts can be anything from round, peeled logs to landscape timbers to ornate mortised-posts. Boards are typically 1×6 to 1×12 inches.

The typical post-and-board fence is 3 to 4 feet high and has three rails. Posts are installed 8 to 12 feet apart depending on the size, weight, and design of the board. The boards are attached to the posts with either lap or mortise joints. Lap joints mean the boards simply butt one another at the post and are nailed to one side of it.

Installing Picket Fences

A picket fence is an ideal compromise between beauty and function. It can both decorate and enclose your yard at low cost. Traditionally, the picket fence reminds us of Colonial architecture, but today's picket fence can be installed around ranch, tudor, split entry, Cape Cod, or most other home styles. This is because of the wide range of picket designs and combinations available. There are literally hundreds of patterns for picket tops including squared ends and bevel ends that produce a simple fence line, to the intricate scroll-sawed gothic, modified gothic, and french gothic patterns. Post caps range from plain flat tops to fancy ornamental shapes such as the acorn, pineapple, and turned goblet.

The typical picket fence is about 36 inches high, and has 3-inch pickets spaced 3 inches apart. Variations abound: 24- to 38-inch picket fences with narrow or broad pickets closely spaced with unique top designs. Color, too, can make picket fences unique.

Picket fences are easy to assemble. You can often purchase precut pickets and post caps that make design a matter of selection. However, if you have a table or radial arm saw, you can construct your own pickets in a short time. Make them out of better grade 1 × 2-, 1 × 3-, or 1 × 4-inch softwoods. Posts are constructed of 2 × 4s and rails of 2 × 3 or 2 × 4s.

Sections of picket fencing can easily be assembled using a 4 × 8 foot sheet of plywood laid across two sawhorses. The thicker the plywood, the easier it will be to nail the pickets to the rails. You can also construct them on a flat driveway. Paint (first coat) your picket fence in sections *before* assembly. Then apply the final coat once the fence is installed. Exterior latex house paint is ideal for covering picket fences.

Post ends should be treated with a high-quality wood preservative, or be built with pressure-treated wood, to ensure a long life. The highest failure rate of wooden fences is just above ground level on posts where rain, snow, and termites can destroy unprotected wood in just a few seasons.

If you're buying prefabricated picket fencing, make sure you can purchase sections that will climb any slopes or drop into any valleys along the fence line. The alternative is to move dirt.

If one of the functions of your picket fence is to keep pets in the yard, consider installing chicken wire or pressure-treated boards underground below the pickets to keep the critters from digging out.

Installing Board Fences

For backyard privacy, nothing beats a tall board fence. It's also easy to build with basic materials and skills. However, the board fence does require more design time because it will become a major part of backyard living. A well-designed board fence can make outdoor rooms within your yard; a poor design becomes a distractive eyesore.

There are many ways to include interest and pattern in your board fence. One popular way to reduce the boxed-in feeling of a board fence is to open up noncritical viewing areas. That is, leave boards off a section or two that opens up a view to a large tree or shrubbery without sacrificing privacy. Boards can be slightly separated to allow some breeze and view through. You can also break the vertical lines of a tall fence with horizontal patterns such as battens, lattice, rails, or even altered designs from top to bottom.

Board fences are very simple to construct: you build a sturdy post and rail frame and then attach the boards. Dimensions vary somewhat around the standard 6-foot boards hung on 2×4 rails between 4×4 posts installed 6 to 8 feet apart. Longer fence runs should have added support or shortened rail spans to make them more secure. Support can come from cross-fencing, a third rail, enlarged post footings, or bracings. Wind and snow can be hazardous to the health of your fence.

Fence boards should be of good quality. Privacy fences should be built with select grades of wood to eliminate loose knots. To eliminate cracks between fence boards, build with tongue and groove or shiplap lumber, or install battens over cracks.

Chain Link Fence

For a strong, practically indestructible fence that requires little maintenance, the chain link fence is your best bet. Compared with other fencing, however, the chain link fence is expensive. Of course, high initial cost is somewhat balanced by the longer life of chain link over wood.

Steel or aluminum chain link fencing is especially good for enclosing yards, play areas, swimming pools, and pet areas. Best of all, the chain link fence can be easily constructed by the do-it-yourselfer with a few basic tools.

Most chain link fences are made with fabric, top rail, line posts, loop caps, terminal posts, tension bar, brace band, rail ends, post caps, gates, and carriage bolts. Tools include a post hole digger, wheelbarrow, shovel and hoe (for cement), tape measure, level, mason's line, pliers, fence stretcher/ block and tackle (can be rented), wrenches, and a hacksaw or pipe cutter.

To install a chain link fence, first calculate the location of terminal (end, corner, and gate) posts. Figure the distance between gate posts by adding the actual width of the gate to an allowance for hinges and latches (3¾ inches for single-walk gates and 5½ inches for double-drive gates).

Mark all posts with crayon or chalk for the correct height of fence you are installing. Terminal posts should be set 2 inches higher and line posts 2 inches lower than the width of the fabric. Set the terminal posts in concrete using a carpenter's level to make sure they are plumb. Crown all post footings for good water drainage.

Next, mark the grade line on all posts measuring from the top down. Then measure the distance between terminal posts and check the line post spacing chart for the exact distance to allow between line posts.

Stretch a mason's line between the outsides of terminal posts. The line posts should be lined up so that when they are set in the center of their holes, their centers will line up with the terminal post centers. When this is done, dig the line post holes and set the line posts.

Move the mason's line up the terminal posts to a point 4 inches below the post tops so that you can align the height of line posts. The post height can be adjusted before the concrete sets up by simply pulling it up or tapping it down. Make sure your moving the line posts does not move them from plumb.

The next step to installing a chain link fence is to apply fittings to terminal posts. Typically this includes (from bottom to top) a tension bar and bands, top rail and rail ends, brace band, and post cap.

After assembling the framework, unroll the chain link fabric on the ground along the fence line starting at a terminal post. Then slide the tension bar through the last link in the fabric and attach this combination to the terminal post using the tension band and bolts provided. The fabric should be on the *outside* face of all posts.

Next, stretch the fabric from the terminal post it's already attached to over the opposite terminal post. Insert the tension bar in the end of the fabric and attach the fence stretcher to the bar. The top of the fabric should be about ½ inch above the top rail to ensure proper height. Once the fabric is sufficiently tight, remove excess fabric and connect the tension bar to the post with tension bands. Then fasten the fabric to the top rail and line posts with tie wires spaced approximately 18 inches apart.

Once the fence is completed, apply male hinges to one of the gate posts, hanging the top hinge upside down to prevent the gate from being lifted off. Loosely apply female hinges to the gate frame and slip them onto the male hinges. Set hinges to allow for full swing of the gate, then align the top of the gate with the top of the fence. Tighten all hinges securely. Finally, install the gate latch.

Installing Decks

If a fence is an outdoor wall, a deck must be an outdoor floor. And just as the floor inside your home can be made of a variety of materials in assorted styles, so can your outdoor deck be constructed in many ways for various purposes.

You've probably had the basic ideas for a deck in your mind for awhile, but maybe they haven't moved to paper yet. This is the time to begin. You can make major changes to your deck *on paper* without additional cost. Later, it becomes more expensive.

First, select the location of your deck by thinking about the *interior* of your house. Locate your deck adjacent to those areas that are most accessible without disrupting interior flow of traffic. Most decks are built next to a front or back entryway. Consider the location of the sun in relation to the deck, especially during the months when you will use the deck the most. Also consider street noise, privacy, and other factors important to your comfort.

Next, estimate approximate size by multiplying the number of people who would normally use it by 20 square feet. That is, if it is primarily a deck for a family of four, an 8 × 10-foot rectangular deck would provide 80 square feet. However, if you plan to have outdoor parties on your deck with up to 20 people, then you'd need 400 square feet—a 20 × 20- or 16 × 25-foot deck. Of course, make sure your deck is scaled to your house. A large deck may overwhelm a small house.

As you're designing and drawing out your deck, keep in mind the capabilities of wood. Use 4 × 4-inch deck posts if your deck is less than 8 feet above ground, and 6 × 6-inch posts if higher. Posts should be pressure-treated lumbers. Other deck wood can be pressure-treated, decay-resistant (such as redwood), or common softwood (pine, fir, hemlock) with a preservative applied after installation. Joists, the horizontal lumber onto which you will nail the decking, should have spans limited by the spacing between the joists. Most decks use 2 × 4s for 16-inch joist span designs; 2 × 6s for 24-inch joist spans; and 2 × 8s for wider spans. However, 2 × 8s have a tendency to warp.

Building Your Deck

The first step to deck construction is to mark the area for your deck with stakes and string (see Figure 10.3).

Deck footings rest on the ground and support the deck posts. Footings may be either concrete blocks, precast pier

FIGURE 10.3 Laying Out a Deck

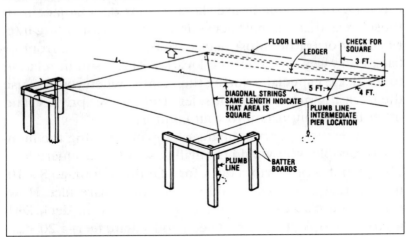

blocks, or poured concrete pads. A footing should be at least twice the size of the post it supports. That is, 4×4-inch posts should rest on 8×8-inch concrete footings.

Deck posts are the vertical members that rest on the footings and support the beams. The length of the posts is important to setting the height of the deck. If your deck must hold large crowds, deep snow, or other heavy loads, or if the deck is quote elevated, use larger posts and cross bracing to prevent lateral movement.

Deck beams rest on the posts and support the joists. For some low decks, beams may rest directly on the footings. Beams of 4×6 inches and greater are common. Beams are often built up from thinner-dimension lumber by fastening them together with bolts or lag screws.

Joists rest on the beams and support the decking. They are installed on edge, with one of the thin sides resting on the beams. At the side of the house, joists may be supported with a ledger. The joist span is determined by the spacing of the joists and the grade of lumber used.

The *decking* is the wood surface on which you will walk. It is installed horizontally on top of the deck joists. Most decking is 2 × 4 or 2 × 6 pressure-treated or decay-resistant wood. Decking should span no more than 24 inches. If you plan to install a large permanent planter, hot tub, spa, or other heavy object, make sure you build in extra support underneath it.

Stairs are made with *treads* and *stringers* (risers). Treads are the stepping surface and are supported by the stringers. Stair treads should be a minimum of 11 inches deep and 6 to 7 inches apart. For wide stairs, notched stringers, placed 24 inches apart, offer enough support. If only two steps are planned, a 2 × 12-inch board can be laid on edge or notched as a stringer. If more steps are needed, a sloping stringer should be used allowing a minimum of 3½ inches below the notch for strength.

Finally, install railings on your deck. Rail posts should be bolted to joists or beams, or be designed as an extension to the deck post.

Installing Outdoor Storage

Just as you have closets, utility rooms, and storage rooms indoors, you can also have storage buildings to contain your outdoor accessories.

A storage building requires careful thought. Begin planning your storage building by developing a list of work areas and storage needs, including automobiles and other vehicles.

As an idea starter, sheds and storage buildings can be constructed to house a garden tractor, gardening tools, power mower and supplies, rakes, brooms, shovels, hoes, axes, lawn trimmers and edgers, wheelbarrows, extension ladders, stepladders, hoses, sprinklers, weed sprayers, insecticides, herbicides, fertilizers, paint, brushes, window-washing equipment, carpenter's tools, storm windows and screens, auto service and repair tools and materials, bicycles, wagon, sleds, skis, canoe, snowmobile, swing and slide set, woodworking shop and equipment, freezer, root vegetables, canned and frozen food, garbage cans, recycled materials, junk, and much more.

Keep in mind as you plan your storage buildings that over the years, your needs will probably change. This year's hobbies and activities may be next year's memories. Also, remember that no matter how much storage space you have, it's not enough. You will soon have it filled. So provide for open, flexible storage buildings that can easily be modified to include or exclude a recreation vehicle, workshop, shelving, or other space-takers.

First, make sure that the outdoor storage unit will be convenient. A few moments of garden work can be done at nearly any time if the tools and materials are nearby, but if the work takes another hour of gathering and putting away materials, the job will probably be put off. Consider installing a small workbench and an area for parts and tools for maintaining equipment.

Safety is another design consideration for storage buildings, especially if children may be around what's stored there. Keep storage buildings securely locked. If the building contains poisons, herbicides, paints, flammable liquids, or other dangerous materials, keep these items locked up separately inside the storage shed.

Remember to plan for adequate lighting so that you won't stumble over materials as you enter from the bright sunlight. Lighting can be provided by windows, skylights, or electrical lights. However, remember that artificial lighting requires that you run electrical service to your storage building at additional effort and cost for minimal use.

How Your Landscaper Can Help

While no contractor likes a "sidewalk supervisor," most will work more conscientiously if they know you're nearby. Also, you might be able to answer a question that will help them do the job faster or more to your liking.

Commonly Asked Questions

Q. What kind of landscaping grows fastest?

A. That depends on where you live and what you consider "fast." Ask your landscape contractor or nursery dealer to recommend fast-growing landscaping for your region. Remember that fast-growing plants can also become overgrown and require more maintenance.

Q. Should I remove an older fence first?

A. In most cases, the best option is to tear out any old fencing and post footings, clear out interfering trees or shrubs, and move large rocks that may interfere with installing your new fence or other outdoor structure.

Q. Would a storage shed be useful or wasteful?

A. A well-designed storage shed is useful if you can find what you need when you need it. Otherwise, it is wasteful.

Using Computers to Help You Remodel

The newest tool in the home remodeling field is the computer.

That's right: the computer. That little machine that the kids have been using to play interactive videogames and surf the Net can be used by those over 21 to get help on remodeling a home.

Your computer can help you design your remodeling jobs, find valuable resources, check out the latest products, get the best financing, and save you money on your remodeling.

This chapter will show you how.

Getting on the Internet

The latest rage is the Internet. Advertisements for products on TV include their "Web address." Friends try to give you their "e-mail address." What does it all mean and, more important, who cares?

179

What does it mean? The terms used are simply words that help describe a new tool, the Internet. It's really no different than any other latest-and-greatest invention in that some people use it for good and others don't. The Internet is nothing to be fearful of. It is simply a tool.

Who cares? Contrary to what many folks say, you *can* live quite well, thank you, without access to the Internet. It is a tool that can help you get information you need faster and, sometimes, easier than in traditional ways. The printed word never replaced conversation as the primary tool of communication. Nor will the Internet replace the printed word.

Maybe the Internet is a tool that can help you remodel your home.

Understanding the Internet

So what is the Internet? It's an *inter*active *net*work of computers connected together through telephone lines. Think of it as a telephone system between computers. One computer calls another to find out what's new. It asks questions, answers questions, and spends a lot of time saying "uh-huh."

What You Need to Get the Internet

What do you need to get on to the Internet? You need a computer, a modem, some communications software called a browser, and a few bucks. The few bucks are to subscribe to an Internet provider or IP. An IP is a service that will connect your computer with other computers on the Internet. The typical monthly charge is less than your cable TV bill. Some IPs charge by the hour and others have a flat monthly fee for unlimited access.

If you want to get on to the Internet, first find a local IP, then ask what software and hardware you'll need. They want you to become a subscriber, so they will typically help you get set up. Where can you find a local IP? Ask at local computer shops, check the classified ads in area news-papers, or ask friends.

☞ **Money-$aving Tip #37** *There's not more than a few hundred dollars difference between fast and super-fast PCs, so get the fastest you can reasonably afford. Also, if you can't see the difference between a $300 monitor and one that costs $1,000, don't buy the expensive one.*

Finding Things on the Internet

There are lots of pieces to the Internet, many of them far beyond the scope of this book. The most popular—and the most friendly—is what's called "the Web." It's also known as the "World Wide Web" or W W W. In fact, many businesses include their web address in advertisements and even on products.

For example, the Web address for the National Association of the Remodeling Industry (NARI) is www.nari.com. What does that mean?

www means it's a World Wide Web address.
nari is the domain name.
com means it is a commercial site (*gov* means government).

There's a bit more to the address, however. To reach this location on the Internet, you need to tell the computer that you're using hypertext transfer protocol. What? Don't worry about it. Just prefix the address with:

http://

So the uniform resource locator (URL) address to reach NARI is:

http://www.nari.com

Type that Web address into your computer and watch the magic start.

Here are some other useful Internet Web addresses to help you remodel your home:

WWW address	*Organization*
http://www.remodelers com	Remodelers Online
http://www.buildandre-model.com	Home Building and Remodeling Resources
http://www.housenet.com	Resources for Do-It-Yourselfers
http://www.protonet.com/sara	Society of American Registered Architects
http://www.woodfloors.org	National Wood Flooring Association
http://www.wwpa.org	Western Wood Products Association
http://www.paint.org	National Paint and Coatings Association
http://www.brickinst.org	Brick Institute of America

Searching the Net

Now that you're plugged in to the Internet, there is much you can look for. Searching, or "surfing," the Internet is relatively easy and there are many tools available. Most Web browser programs offer you ways to search the Internet for key words.

The problem will soon become not how to find things on the Internet, but how to *selectively* find things. For example, asking for a search of the Internet using the term "remodel" finds literally thousands of Web addresses where the term is used. With practice and by reading the "help" screens, you'll soon learn how to find what you're looking for.

Corresponding on the Net

Once on the Internet, you'll meet people and find a few new and old friends. How can you correspond with them?

By using electronic mail, or e-mail. Web browser programs usually have some type of e-mail writing and delivery system on them. Your IP can tell you more. In fact, your IP can give you an e-mail address.

For example, if your commercial Internet provider is named Harborside and your account name with them is Cottage, your e-mail address will probably be:

cottage@harborside.com

Folks who want to send you a message would do so using your e-mail address. And you would use their e-mail address to send them a message. It's like your street address or telephone number, except it's an electronic address.

Using Other Online Services

The Internet is a big network that nobody really owns or manages. You buy access time from those who supply the computer hardware and buy the telephone time to get on the Internet. There are, however, many commercial networks called online services.

The two most popular online services with consumers today are America Online (800-316-6633) and Compuserve (800-848-8199). Not only do they offer their own electronic resources, but both also offer access to the Internet.

How Your Remodeler Can Help

Chances are your remodeling contractor already has a computer with software programs to design and manage projects. Depending on compatibility, you may be able to make some preliminary designs with a low-cost program, then export them into your contractor's program, saving work.

Commonly Asked Questions

Q. Can someone on the Internet access my computer?

A. Not without knowing your passwords. If security is a concern, make sure your communications software and modem offer password protection. And make sure you don't give out your password to others.

Q. How can I get information off the Internet?

A. Most Web browser software includes features to let you download files or print information directly from the screen to your local provider. They use programs called file transfer protocol or FTP.

Q. What are newsgroups?

A. Newsgroups are groups of people who exchange information and chat among themselves on a common topic. There are newsgroups for homeowners, do-it-yourselfers, remodelers, contractors, and thousands of other topics. To learn more about newsgroups, talk with your Internet provider.

Resources for Remodelers

There are many valuable associations, books, video-tapes, and magazines that will help you plan and tackle your remodeling project. They include:

- Time-Life (800-621-7026) and others offer excellent books and videos on aspects of home remodeling and repair.
- Craftsman Book Company (800-829-8123) publishes books on home construction and remodeling skills.
- *The New Complete Home Repair Manual* by the Editors of Consumer Guide (847-676-3470).
- Popular magazines include *Better Homes and Gardens*, *Home Magazine*, *Popular Mechanics*, *Home Mechanics*, and others on most larger newsstands.
- Also watch network and cable TV programs like *Home-time* and *This Old House,* as well as the Home and Garden Network for ideas and information on remodeling.

Other valuable resources for remodelers include:

American Institute of Architects
1735 New York Avenue, N.W.
Washington, DC 20006
202-626-7300

American Institute of Contractors
10554 Cypress Way, Suite F
Cypress, CA 90630
714-828-8271

American Lighting Association
435 N. Michigan Avenue, #1717
Chicago, IL 60611
312-644-0828

American Society of Interior Designers
608 Massachusetts Avenue, N.E.
Washington, DC 20002
202-546-3480

American Subcontractors Association
1004 Duke Street
Alexandria, VA 22314
703-684-3450

Crawford's Old House Store
550 Elizabeth Street, #105
Waukesha, WI 53186
800-556-7878

Home Improvement Research Institute
400 Knightsbridge Parkway
Lincolnshire, IL 60069
800-621-2845

Independent Contractors Association
6400 Woodward Avenue
Downers Grove, IL 60516
630-971-0102

International Remodeling Contractors Association
One Regency Drive
Bloomfield, CT 06002
860-242-6823

Kitchen Cabinet Manufacturers Association
1899 Preston White Drive
Reston, VA 22091
703-264-1690

Mortgage Bankers Association of America
1125 15th Street, N.W.
Washington, DC 20005
202-861-6500

**National Association of Home Builders—
  Remodelers Council**
1201 15th Street, N.W.
Washington, DC 20005
800-368-5242

National Association of Real Estate Appraisers
8383 E. Evans Road
Scottsdale, AZ 85260
602-948-8000

National Association of the Remodeling Industry
4301 N. Fairfax Drive, Suite 310
Arlington, VA 22203
703-276-7600

National Housewares Manufacturers Association
6400 Shafer Court, #650
Rosemont, IL 60018
847-292-4200

National Kitchen & Bath Association
687 Willow Grove Street
Hackettstown, NJ 07840
908-852-0033

National Paint and Coatings Association
1500 Rhode Island Avenue, N.W.
Washington, DC 20005
202-462-6272

National Roofing Contractors Association
10255 W. Higgins, #600
Rosemont, IL 60018
847-299-9070

Painting & Decorating Contractors of America
3913 Old Lee Highway
Fairfax, VA 22030
703-359-0826

Title One Home Improvement Lenders Association
1726 18th Street, N.W.
Washington, DC 20009
202-328-1671

Robinson's Wall Coverings
225 W. Spring Street
Titusville, PA 16354
800-458-2426

GLOSSARY

A-C exterior An exterior-type sanded plywood panel with A-grade face, C-grade, back and C-grade inner plies bonded with exterior glue. Commonly used for fences, farm buildings, soffits, and other high-moisture applications where the appearance or smoothness of only one side is important.

acrylic resin An ingredient of water-base (latex) paints and stains. A synthetic resin with excellent weathering characteristics. Acrylics can be colorless and transparent, or pigmented.

air-dried lumber Lumber that has been dried naturally by air and with a minimum moisture content of 12 to 20 percent.

anchor bolts Bolts to secure a wooden sill plate to concrete or masonry patio or foundation.

apron The flat member of the inside trim of a window that is placed against the wall immediately beneath the stool.

areaway An open subsurface space adjacent to a building that is used to admit light or air or as a means of access to a basement.

astrogal A molding attached to one of a pair of swinging doors against which the other door strikes.

backband A simple molding sometimes used around the outer edge of plain rectangular casing as a decorative feature.

batten Narrow strips of wood used to cover joints or as decorative vertical members over wide boards, such as on deck rails or fences.

beam A structural member that transversely supports a load. Deck beams are typically 2×8, 2×10, or 2×12 inches in size.

bearing wall A wall that supports any vertical load in addition to its own weight.

bevel To cut panel or wood edges or ends at an angle to make smooth mating joints.

blind nailing Nailing in such a way that the nailheads are not visible on the face of the work. They are usually placed at the tongue of matched boards.

189

blind stop A rectangular molding, usually ¾ by 1⅜ inches or more in width, that is used in the assembly of a window frame. It serves as a stop for storm and screen or combination windows and to resist air infiltration.

blocking Light lumber strips nailed between major framing members to support edges of structural units where they meet.

board foot Unit of measuring lumber. Theoretically, a board measuring 1 square foot on the surface and 1-inch thick, it is usually 144 square inches and 13⁄16-inch thick.

boards Yard lumber less than 2 inches thick and 2 or more inches wide. Most commonly used for fencing and decks.

box beam A beam built of lumber and plywood in the form of a long hollow box that will support more load across an opening than will its individual members alone.

brace An inclined piece of lumber applied to a wall of fence section to stiffen the structure. Often used as temporary bracing until framing has been completed.

bridging Short wood or metal braces or struts placed crosswise between joists to help keep them in alignment. Bridging may be solid or crossed struts.

buck Often used in reference to rough frame opening members. Door bucks used in reference to metal door frames.

butt joint The junction where the ends of two timbers or other members meet in a square-cut joint.

cap The upper member of a column, pilaster, door cornice, molding, and the like.

casement frames and sash Frames of wood or metal that enclose part or all of the sash, which may be opened by hinges affixed to the vertical edges.

casing Molding of various widths and thicknesses that is used to trim door and window openings at the jambs.

caulk Weather sealant used to fill joints or seams. Caulks are available as putties, ropes, or compounds extruded from cartridges.

checking Wood exposed to alternating moist and dry conditions eventually develops open cracks, or checks. Reduce checking by sealing panel edges before installation to minimize moisture absorption, and by using a priming coat or resin sealer on the surfaces.

clear span Distance between inside faces of supports.

concrete form Mold in which concrete is poured to set.

concrete, plain Concrete either without reinforcement, or reinforced only for shrinkage or temperature change.

condensation Beads or drops of water, and frequently frost in extremely cold weather, that accumulates on the inside of the exterior covering of a building when warm, moisture-laden air from the interior reaches a point where the temperature permits the air to sustain the moisture it holds. Use of louvers or attic ventilators will reduce moisture condensation in attics. A vapor barrier under the gypsum lath or drywall on exposed walls will reduce condensation in them.

corner braces Diagonal braces at the corners of frame structures to stiffen and strengthen the structure.

course A layer of bricks or shingles.

crawl space A space about 2 feet high beneath a structure allowing access to plumbing and wiring, normally enclosed by the foundation wall.

cripple Any vertical framing member cut less than full length.

crosscutting Sawing wood across the grain.

d Penny, a measurement of nail sizes. Originated as the price per hundred nails.

dado A rectangular groove across the width of a board or plank. In interior decoration, a special type of wall treatment.

deck paint An enamel with a high degree of resistance to mechanical wear and designed for use on deck and porch floors.

decking The boards used for the floor surface of the deck. Decking is nailed to the joists. Typical decking is 2×4-, 2×6-, or 2×10-inch boards.

direct nailing To nail perpendicular to the initial surface or to the junction of the pieces jointed. Also called face nailing.

door jamb, interior The surrounding case into which and out of which a door closes and opens. It consists of two upright pieces called side jambs and a horizontal head jamb.

dormer An opening in a sloping roof, the framing of which projects out to form a vertical wall suitable for windows or other openings.

drip cap A molding placed on the exterior top side of a door or window frame to cause water drip beyond the outside of the frame.

eave The edge of a roof that extends beyond or overhangs a wall. The underside of an eave may form an open soffit.

expansion joint Open joints between sections of concrete to allow for expansion and contraction.

exterior glue A fully waterproof adhesive used in exterior paneling.

face The highest-grade side of any veneer-faced panel that has outer plies of different veneer grades. Example: C side of a C-D exterior grade plywood.

fascia Wood or plywood trim used along the edge of the deck to provide a decorative edge.

filler A material for filling nail holes, checks, cracks, or other blemishes in wood surfaces before application of paint, varnish, or other finishes.

fire-stop A solid, tight closure of a concealed space placed to prevent the spread of fire and smoke through such a space. In a frame wall, this will usually consist of 2 × 4 cross-blocking between studs.

flagstone Flat stones 1 to 4 inches thick used for rustic patios, walks, and steps.

footing The base for deck posts and other structural members. The footing is two to three times wider than the member it supports, and distributes the weight of the structure to the ground over a larger area to prevent settling.

frame construction Construction in which the structural parts are wood or dependent on a wood framework for support. Typically, lumber framing is sheathed with structural wood panels for roofs, walls, and floors.

framing, balloon A system of framing a building in which all vertical structural elements of the bearing walls and all partitions consist of single pieces extending from the top of the foundation sill plate to the roof plate and to which all floor joists are fastened.

framing, platform A system of framing a building in which floor joists of each story are below or on the foundation sill for the first story, and the bearing walls and partitions rest on the subfloor of each story.

frost line The depth of frost penetration in the soil. This depth varies in different parts of the country. Fence footings should be placed below this depth to prevent movement.

furring Process of leveling parts of a ceiling, wall, or floor by means of wood strips, called furring strips, before adding panel cover.

glue Adhesives designed to produce sturdier joints when combined with other fasteners. Type depends on purpose and exposure of the finished product.

grain The direction, size, arrangement, appearance, or quality of fibers in wood.

grain, edge (vertical) Edge-grain lumber has been sawed parallel to the pith of the log and approximately at right angles to the growth rings (i.e., the rings form an angle of 45 degrees or more with the surface of the piece).

grain, flat Flat-grain lumber has been sawed parallel to the pith of the log and approximately tangent to the growth rings (i.e., the rings form an angle of less than 45 degrees with the surface of the piece).

grain, quartersawed Another term for edge grain.

gusset plate A piece of wood connecting lumber members of a truss or other frame structure. Gussets may be applied to one or both sides of the joint.

header A beam placed perpendicular to joists and to which joists are nailed in framing for chimney, stairway, door, or windows. Also, a wooden lintel.

heartwood The wood extending from the pith to the sapwood, the cells of which no longer participate in the life process of the tree.

I-beam A steel beam with a cross-section resembling the letter I. It is used for long spans as basement beams or over wide wall openings, such as a double-car garage.

insulation, thermal Any material high in resistance to heat transmission that, when placed in the walls, ceiling, or floors of a structure, will reduce the rate of heat flow.

jamb The side and head lining of a doorway, window, or other opening.

joist Horizontal framing member of a deck, floor, or ceiling. Deck joists are typically 2×8, 2×10, or 2×12 lumber.

kiln-dried lumber Lumber that has been kiln dried, often to a moisture content of 6 to 12 percent. Common varieties of softwood lumber, such as framing lumber, are dried to a somewhat higher moisture content.

lattice A framework of crossed wood or metal strips.

lumber, boards Yard lumber less than 2 inches thick and 2 inches or more wide.

lumber, dimension Yard lumber from 2 inches to, but not including, 5 inches thick and 2 inches or more wide. It includes joists, rafters, studs, planks, and small timbers.

lumber, dressed size The dimension of lumber after shrinking from green dimension and after machining to size or pattern.

lumber, matched Lumber that is dressed and shaped on one edge in a grooved pattern and on the other in a tongued pattern.

lumber, shiplap Lumber that is edge-dressed to make a close rabbeted or lapped joint.

millwork Generally, all building materials made of finished wood and manufactured in millwork plants and planing mills are known as millwork. Such items include inside and outside doors, window and door frames, blinks, porchwork, mantels, panelwork, stairways, moldings, and interior trim. Millwork normally does not include flooring, ceilings, or siding.

miter joint The joint of two pieces at an angle that bisects the joining angle. For example, the miter joint at the side and head casing at a door opening is made at a 45 degree angle.

moisture content of wood Weight of the water contained in the wood, usually expressed as a percentage of the weight of the oven-dried wood.

molding A wooden strip that has a curved or projecting surface and is used for decorative purpose.

mullion Vertical bar or divider in the frame between windows, doors, and other openings.

muntin A small member that divides the glass or openings of sash or doors.

natural finish A transparent finish that does not seriously alter the original color or grain of the natural wood. Natural finishes are usually provided by sealers, oils, varnishes, water-repellent preservatives, and other similar materials.

nominal dimension Full designated dimension. For example, a nominal 2 × 4-inch stud may measure 1½ × 3½ inches when surfaced.

o.c., or on center The measurement of spacing for studs, rafters, joists, and posts, from the center of one member to the center of the next.

parting stop or strip A small wooden piece used in the side and head jambs of double-hung windows to separate the upper and lower sashes.

pier A column of masonry, usually rectangular, used to support other structural members. Often used as support under decks.

pitch The slope of a surface, such as a roof or the ground.

plate In wood frame construction, the horizontal lumber member on top and/or bottom of the exterior wall studs that ties those studs together and supports the studs or rafters.

plumb Exactly perpendicular; vertical.

plywood A piece of wood made of three or greater odd number of layers of veneer joined with glue and usually laid with the grain of adjoining plies at right angles.

post Vertical supporting members that rest on the pier blocks or foundation and provide support for the beams. Deck posts are typically 4×4 or 6×6 lumber.

preservative Any substance that, for a reasonable length of time, will prevent the action of wood-destroying fungi, borers of various kinds, and similar destructive agents when the wood has been properly coated or impregnated with it.

pressure-treated lumber Wood treated with preservative or fire retardants by pressure-injecting treating solutions into wood cells.

purlin Subframing that supports roof decking where larger beams are main structural supports.

quarter-round A small molding that has the cross-section of a quarter circle.

rabbet A rectangular longitudinal groove that is cut in the corner edge of a board or plank.

rafter Supporting member of a roof immediately beneath the sheathing.

rail The cross members of panel doors or of a sash. Also, the upper and lower members of a balustrade or staircase that extends from one vertical support, such as a post, to another.

ridge beam The top horizontal member of a sloping roof, against which the ends of the rafters are fixed or supported.

run In stairs, the net width of a stem or the horizontal distance covered by a flight of stairs.

sapwood The outer zone of wood, next to the bark. In the living tree it contains some living cells, as well as dead and dying cells. In most species, it is lighter colored than the heartwood. In all species, it is lacking in decay resistance.

sash A single window frame that contains one or more panes of glass.

sash balance A device that is usually operated by a spring or tensioned weatherstripping designed to counterbalance a double-hung window sash.

sealer A finishing material, either clear or pigmented, that is usually applied directly over uncoated wood for the purpose of sealing the surface.

seasoning Removal of moisture from wood to improve its serviceability, usually by air drying (drying by air exposure without artificial heat) or kiln drying (drying in a kiln with artificial heat).

sheathing The structural covering on the outside surfaces of framing providing support for construction, snow, and wind loads and backing for attaching exterior facing materials such as wall siding, roof shingles, or underlayment in double-layer floors.

sill The member forming the lower side of an opening, such as a doorsill, windowsill, etc.

sill plate The lowest framing member of a structure, resting on the foundation and supporting the floor system and the uprights of the frame.

square A unit of measure, 100 square feet, usually applied to roofing material.

stile An upright framing member in a panel door.

stringer A lumber member supporting a series of cross members; commonly used in constructing stairs.

stud The basic vertical framing members of walls, usually 2 × 4 inches nominal, traditionally spaced 16 inches on center in residential and 24 inches on center in storage buildings.

subfloor Boards or plywood laid on joists over which a finish floor is to be laid.

termite shield A metal shield placed in or on a foundation or masonry wall or around pipes to prevent passage of termites.

toenailing To drive a nail at a slant with the initial surface in order to permit it to penetrate into a second member.

tongue-and-groove joint A system for jointing in which the tongue or rib of one member fits exactly into the groove of another.

trim The finish materials in a building, such as moldings, that are applied around openings (window trim, door trim) or at the floor and ceiling of rooms (baseboard, cornice, and other moldings).

truss A combination of members usually arranged in triangular units to form a rigid framework for supporting loads over a span. Parallel chord trusses are also used for floor and roof supports.

vapor barrier Material used to retard the movement of water vapor through walls and to prevent condensation in walls. It usually has a perm value of less than 1/0 and is applied separately over the warm side of exposed walls or as a part of batt or blanket insulation.

water-repellent preservative A liquid designed to penetrate into wood and impart water repellency and a moderate preservative protection. It is used for millwork, such as sashes and frames, and is usually applied by dipping.

INDEX

197

ABOUT THE AUTHORS

The CENTURY 21® System, recognized as the number-one consumer brand in real estate, has helped millions of people with their homebuying and homeselling needs for more than 25 years. In the relocation process as well, the CENTURY 21® System has assisted families every step of the way.

To meet the high expectations of today's demanding, value-conscious consumer, the CENTURY 21® System has redefined the real estate industry with innovative technology tools, strategic alliances with other industry leaders that offer a wide array of home-oriented products and services, distinct brands for special properties, and other housing-related opportunities.

Visit the CENTURY 21® System at *Century 21 Communities^{SM},* the most comprehensive source of real estate and community information on cities across North America, on America Online® at **Keyword: CENTURY 21.** Or contact one of the System's network of 6,400 independently owned and operated offices throughout the United States and Canada, as well as in 21 countries around the world.

Dan Ramsey is the author of *CENTURY 21® Guide to Remodeling Your Home* and more than two dozen other books for homeowners and do-it-yourselfers. In addition, Dan has broad experience in the construction industry and is a member of the National Association of Home and Workshop Writers. He is also the consultant and contributing editor for Consumer Guide's *New Complete Home Repair Manual.*